Mentoring Human Potential

Mentoring Human Potential

Student Peer Mentors as Catalysts for Academic Success

SCOTT SELDIN

with a Foreword by Dr. Bradford Keeney

iUniverse, Inc.
Bloomington

Mentoring Human Potential
Student Peer Mentors as Catalysts for Academic Success

iUniverse books may be ordered through booksellers or by contacting:

iUniverse
1663 Liberty Drive
Bloomington, IN 47403
www.iuniverse.com
1-800-Authors (1-800-288-4677)

ISBN: 978-1-4620-4019-3 (sc)
ISBN: 978-1-4620-4020-9 (e)

iUniverse rev. date: 11/15/2011

CONTENTS

This book is lovingly dedicated to my parents, Rose and Joseph Seldin, mentors extraordinaire, whose wisdom I see reflected in my son Jasper's eyes.

For Jasper and Sandra

In every human being, a divine spark

—Fyodor Dostoevsky

Foreword

Dr. Bradford Keeney, psychologist, author

In the pages that follow, Scott Seldin will lead you toward the ways that mentor and mentee can open themselves to being moved by Spirit. He will courageously point the way to the greater mysteries that bless those who dare enter with an open heart. In Spirit, we find the soulful life and the path worth living and dying for. I encourage you to trust his guiding voice and to reorient the way in which mystery rather than understanding, spirit rather than motivation, and love rather than reason can be the pillars of guidance in your everyday life.

All relationships, whether mentor and mentee, friends, mates, or partners, require openness to Spirit in order to become filled with vitality, imagination, and charged mission. Spirit, the mystery that infuses life into all that it breathes, is freely available to everyone. When mentor and mentee submit themselves in an open and good way to being moved by a mind greater than their psychological selves, Spirit takes notice and enters the scene.

The openness that opens this door is sincere humility, an acknowledgment that both mentor and mentee can be part of something greater than their understanding and larger than the particulars of their situation and moment. The door opens wider when humor and play become part of the dialogue. They further attract Spirit and help lubricate the cogs of creative process.

Spirit, mystery, humility, play, and humor are all members of the same family. In their matrix, we find the direction we have been seeking, the intuitions that start us anew, and the creative inspiration that readies us for the next challenge.

PREFACE

Spirit in the Making

I was born in Brooklyn, New York, and my first year on earth imprinted more concrete and bricks than green leafy trees, though there were trees on the block where I lived.

My family stayed summer weekends in a cabin perched atop a steep overgrown hillside on the outskirts of Peekskill, New York. A dirt road led to the cabin, cutting through tall grass and wildflowers. In this paradise, an unnamed spirit surrounded me and became me.

In one of my earliest memories, a summery weekend morning, my mother and I made our way down wooden steps leading to a brook. She dipped a large metal cup into the water and showed me several minnows swimming in the cup's brook water.

I thrilled to see life swimming as minnows in a cup of brook. There was no separation between the world at large and myself. I saw and felt the same aliveness and life everywhere I looked—in the trees, the rabbits, bugs, snakes, and butterflies. I was delighted by everything that walked, crawled, flew, or grew in the ground. I was connected.

We left Brooklyn when I was five and I grew up in a one hundred and fifty-year-old former Quaker meeting house in Croton-on-Hudson, New York. Seventy-five years after it was built, the meeting house became a one-room schoolhouse.

During one very cold winter, my mother decided to change our living room wallpaper. When the old wallpaper on one wall was peeled off, my father found a dusty green blackboard underneath. My mother delighted in exposing the blackboard on the wall and decided not to cover it up with new wallpaper. We all wrote messages with chalk on the board. The fireplace flickered on the old green blackboard through the longest winter I've ever known.

I had written my name on the top center—Mr. Seldin. I underlined my name and sat underneath it, imagining I was the teacher, home schooling in that one room schoolhouse of ten or fifteen kids sitting at small wooden desks, like the weathered one I found on our land.

We were snowed in for several days and I imagined kids trapped inside, just like me, noses pressed up against the window, the snow too forbidding to go out and play.

My brothers and I played cards and board games and my father told me stories about the schoolhouse and the children who went there who were members of a small and tight Croton community, an extended family depending on each other, a touch of Americana.

The weather broke and I went back to school. My mother found new wallpaper and changed her mind about the old blackboard and it disappeared again for decades to come. It disappeared but something in me was awakened. I was to become an educator and my upbringing was ideally suited for my dream.

My parents imbued our family with ethics, empathy, compassion, reverence for life, and a desire to help repair the world. I was raised with spirit through daily, untrumpeted acts of kindness and generosity. Both my parents were mentors, actively helping to make a better world for their children, their friends, their community, and the world at large. I was lucky. I had great parents and two great brothers, and because of this I made a practice of relating to everything and everyone as a manifestation of the same divine consciousness.

Acknowledgments

I am grateful for the contributions to *Mentoring Human Potential* made by Dr. Bradford Keeney; Dr. Rey Carr; Susanne Benton, my inspiring editor; mentors and mentees; Debora Bluestone, text design; and those who have guided me toward my highest potential.

INTRODUCTION

The inspiration to write this book came after a workshop I gave at an international conference, Improving University Teaching, held in Jaen, Spain. Educators had gathered from all over the world to learn about cutting edge ideas that would benefit their students.

My workshop, "Student Peer Mentoring: a Holistic Approach," sparked insightful discussion. Without exception, this extraordinary and diverse group saw the same positive value in peer mentoring that I did, and several asked me to help establish programs at their colleges.

I teach mentoring as a protected, supportive, mutually trusting, spirit-infused relationship between a guiding individual who shares experience, wisdom, knowledge, insight, and perspective with another individual who is committed to learn, evolve, and develop potential skills. These educators were particularly interested in the role spirit plays in a holistic approach to education. When I talked about mind, body, and spirit, they responded with great spirit of their own, and their enthusiasm re-ignited my own enthusiasm and spirit.

Flying home to the United States from Spain, I thought about the profound philosophy of kindness and encouragement underpinning all good mentoring relationships, and before my plane touched down I decided to write this book about holistic student peer mentoring. Among my book's goals is to break through any taboo about exploring spirit as a beneficial resource for academic success. My approach is unambiguous.

Mentoring Human Potential is a manual for mentoring and being mentored from the miracle within, where learning blooms through the powerful expression of spirit. To mentor from within, mentors should experience and communicate from the timeless center of all beings, where the breath of life dwells most freely and can guide most easily. The timeless center is the present moment, the only moment that has ever existed.

We are all miracles, each of us stunningly complex and mysterious, regardless of IQ and everyday abilities. The life force within us all, this little light of mine and yours, is the light within each of our many-quintillion-member family of life on earth. We are all miracles, turning in perfect orbit around our life-giving sun. Experiencing this reality with everyday awareness helps summon the energy, dedication, and purpose needed to achieve our potential as students and as human beings.

This perspective is an important one to experience when mentoring. Honoring our shared miracle each day honors a powerful source of motivation, a source that engenders humility, gratitude, and a desire to not waste the gift of life.

It has been said there are only two ways to live your life: as though nothing is a miracle, or as though everything is a miracle. I choose to live my life as though everything is a miracle. This is the perspective I ask mentors and mentees to consider when mentoring or being mentored.

Witness the miracle. We blink into existence, into the arms of loving parents (if we're lucky), nurtured through our early years with tender care and a growing trust that our survival needs will be met. As babies and as young children, we internalize the human clock, habits, values, and emotional range of those around us. We imprint their catalysts for happiness and unhappiness, their judgments and responses to frustration, their fears and daydreams. Our first mentors are family members who model ways of being in the world, which is why every parent or guardian has the potential to mentor with spirit.

If students are lucky enough to have had a few great mentors in the years leading to their first day at college, a student peer mentoring program is an opportunity to extend and deepen the teachings of former mentors, expanding their teachings with spirit. And if they didn't have great mentors, mentoring can provide someone to help them successfully discover and blaze their own trails.

Mentoring programs can help students explore and achieve their academic and human potential, their spirited potential, and it is with this in mind that I share my experiences creating and supervising a student peer mentoring program.

CHAPTER ONE

Mentoring with Spirit and a Shared Goal— Graduation

Are you thinking of starting a student peer mentoring program? Becoming a mentor? A mentee? Don't subjugate spirit, that which shines through existence, simply because mind-centered academic life separates itself from it, claiming to be holistic but focusing almost exclusively on mind, with body a distant second and spirit barely mentioned.

A central thesis of this book is that spirit, personally defined, is an ally in waiting for every student—thus the depth of ruminations about our shared, inspiriting source as a powerful resource to help achieve educational goals. My thesis is field-tested and well worth extended discourse, it is that important to the education of every student regardless of educational level.

If you are thinking of supervising a mentoring program, this book will lead you from your intention to a commitment to set up a program and run it with spirit as the wind at your sails. Inspirited, directed intention gathers energy and a commitment to itself—a process you will want to initiate in all your mentors and mentees. As supervisor, though, you are also mentor for mentors in your program. Therefore, read *Mentoring Human Potential* as both supervisor and mentor.

If you are thinking of becoming a mentor, this book will give you the inspiration and tools you will need to transform the lives of your mentees, as well as your own life. Spirit is intention's trusted guide. Have clarity about your intention—to help others achieve their educational dream, graduation, or to graduate yourself—and that which is boundless will bolster your efforts, helping you and everyone in your mentoring program achieve academic goals, most importantly, graduation.

And yes, if you are thinking of becoming a mentee, you will learn how to use your intention to be a successful mentee who will eventually self-mentor and, it is hoped, mentor others.

EXPERIENCE SPIRIT

My mentor training emphasizes the needed balance of mind, body, and spirit. Post-training, because spirit is routinely neglected in academic life, mentors often ask me questions about accessing their power within. They want help exploring what their animating essence means to them personally, and how they can align themselves with this energy, which will guide, revitalize, and motivate them when mentoring or being mentored.

The first thing I tell them is we all work with spirit every day. Noticing it in our daily life is key. It's not a trick, it's not a secret. It's human spirit. Come with empathy and an open heart and it will be revealed. We all connect in a unique way.

If your method is to sit quietly next to a fountain listening to running water, freeing your mind from negative, distracting thoughts, do so as a regular practice. Some prefer formal methods, e.g., meditation or prayer, while others prefer informal methods, such as music, cooking, exercise, or a walk in nature. The goal is the same—to quiet and focus one's mind.

As elders revered for their wisdom have said, "Live in spirit and spirit will live in you." Our inscrutable universe provides as many methods for accessing spirit as there are students.

My student peer mentoring program has led mentors and mentees to examine the role of spirit in their lives, which has helped them develop the sustaining will and perseverance needed for academic success.

Mentors ask me, "If spirit is an invisible force made visible in our life, how do we help make it visible?" I tell them we do so by drawing forth spirit's elevating life force, manifesting it through the best effort we have in us. That which is the presence of the present moment, when consciously embraced, enhances a student's potential for academic success.

Mentors ask, "How do I know if I'm experiencing spirit?" I answer their question with a question: "How alive do you feel inside?"

Countless discoveries, inventions, and success stories have been the result of a deep reaching within for the pluck, passion, and energy that draw us/spirit toward our most compelling goals and dreams.

People, spirited, have made the impossible possible using the power of positive, expansive thinking and strong, imaginative wills, imagining it and making it so.

That which cannot be bought or sold is in the spring of our step, it's in a smile, or a kindness passed along. Just as we shrink or distance ourselves from negativity, we lean toward good. It's simple . . . just begin. See where you are and take it from there. Have clarity of purpose every day, keeping mind, body, and spirit in harmonious, intentional relationship, honoring each of these intertwined aspects of human existence.

By the end of the semester's second week, my mentors are telling me where they are with spirit and where they think their mentees are. With a new enthusiasm and openness, they and their mentees understand what they need to learn and do to achieve their potential as students and how to go about it.

EXPERIENCE SPIRIT AS RESILIENCY

Though humans are remarkably resilient by nature, our ability to spring back from adversity is more pronounced in some than others. For almost all college students, handling the academic and social pressures of college life is a daily challenge. Resiliency is a vital asset.

What determines who can handle the pressures of academic and social life and who can't? Why is it that some students navigate demands and difficulties well, from a calm center, telling themselves "You can handle this," while others self-talk, "You can't handle this," and fall apart?

What fosters resiliency? Students are better able to recover from setbacks and adversity when they perceive themselves through their strengths, rather than their weaknesses. Their strengths give them the inner confidence needed to adapt successfully to times when their life path is barbed.

Program supervisors and mentors, though your mentees have academic weaknesses, relate to them through their strengths while strengthening their weaknesses. Perceive them through the wholeness of their resilient spirits. Recognize and honor their accomplishments, talents, and complexity as human beings with remarkable potential.

My mentoring programs strengthen resiliency in mentees by strengthening their belief in themselves. Resiliency—the ability to do the mile, go the distance—takes a certain amount of faith, if only in one's self, to cross the finish line.

Mentoring programs help students develop faith and protective factors, e.g., caring relationships, problem solving skills, sharpened learning and study strategies, self-advocacy, and self-management. These protective factors help create meaningful involvement and confidence in their decision-making abilities. When we live intentionally in mind, body, and spirit, resiliency is a natural byproduct.

THE ROAD TO GRADUATION

It is easy to disconnect from that which is the light in every shadow. During my more than twenty years in higher education I have seen good, strong, smart people have difficulties that have ruined their academic semester. I've seen them

- psychologically immobilized by and/or under-prepared for the academic and personal challenges of college life
- stressed and dysfunctional because of difficulty connecting with peers, professors, or family members
- lacking motivation to study and/or socialize
- troubled by significant personal losses or turmoil from a life change such as the transition from home to a college far away from family and friends
- thrown off balance by a dating relationship gone south or a friendship betrayed
- disturbed by a shifting or conflicted sense of personal identity

or simply missing their cat.

The road to graduation can be rocky, often in unexpected ways. No one is immune to becoming overwhelmed by a combination of social, academic, and/or financial problems. Usually we work through these challenges, but on occasion I see students who clearly need more help than the mentoring program can provide. I ask if they think counseling would help. If they say "yes," I guide them to our counseling center and they work it through.

Most of the students you will work with won't need counseling; they need a student peer mentoring program. Comprehensive mentoring of mind, body, and spirit works. I have letters from grateful, relieved parents that tell me their kids would not have graduated without this program and my guidance. I have testimonies from students who tell me their success and ability to stay in school was predicated on their ability to have a student peer mentor. The program helps students achieve their potential and graduate.

The meaning of a college degree is personal *and* universal. Graduation is a golden door to a desired life, however that life might be imagined. And yet, despite the importance of graduation, it is a beacon that can dim, all but unseen when everyday challenges dominate the thoughts of a student.

From time to time, remind your mentees of the powerful goal you share—graduation. When this inspiring goal is awakened in students, they are more willing to commit the time and energy and make the sacrifices necessary to receive a college degree. The goal of graduation helps students tackle schoolwork with increased energy, concentration, and sense of purpose.

With graduation in mind, bring out the best in yourself and your mentees. Work with what *is*. Work enthusiastically, approvingly, and always respect the student you are mentoring. You share the same human condition, the same potential for self-discovery and personal happiness. This understanding is foundational for effective mentoring and when conveyed over time to students, the results are remarkable.

I experienced just how remarkable the results can be when I gave a workshop at Heart of Los Angeles Youth (HOLA), an extraordinary community-supported organization for at-risk young people. My workshop, "How to Have a Successful First Year at College," included a discussion of spirit and how to balance mind, body, and spirit so they would graduate again, next time from college.

After my workshop, a high school senior from an inner city high school told me, "You believe in us the way HOLA staff believe in us. They've kept us from dropping out, kept us working toward our goal—to graduate and go to college. They've had success with all of us."

The graduating seniors in my workshop who had been mentored by HOLA's caring and wise staff carried the staff's collective spirit within them. Staff believed in them through the years and now they believed in themselves. They were all going to a college in the fall, fulfilling HOLA's central mission. This is mentoring at its best.

AN UNMATCHED SOURCE

Mentors, to serve our common purpose, graduation, guide your mentees with *joie de vivre*, whether perceived to be animated by a higher power beyond mind, or simply a desire to serve others in a selfless way, giving back to a world that has given so much. Either way, the life force within serves our highest good. As you give you also receive, yielding prosperity for all.

Have the courage to behold and celebrate that which cannot be explained, that which is limited only by the consciousness in which it dwells. Behold the energy of the universe yearning to fulfill and express its potential. Is there anything more mysterious and magical than spirit as it embodies a universe with its eternal presence of love and light?

Because paths to shared beingness are many and rich with opportunity for wise inner motivation and guidance, the timeless Now, by its nature, serves the highest good, whatever the situation, whatever the path. For mentors and mentees, that which is inner wisdom can provide an unmatched source of strength and motivation.

THE RELATIONSHIP OF SPIRIT AND HARD WORK

Mentors and mentees, draw upon spirit's life force within to help you be the strength, inspiration, and dedication needed to achieve each day's potential and the ultimate goal—graduation. But know that in addition to spirit, academic success will require sustained effort, self-discipline, and a positive mind-set. Though academic and social challenges may be formidable, success is within reach of proactive students (including all mentors and mentees) who get the help they need, and work hard.

The life lesson found in the relationship of spirit and hard work is profound. While spirit, the breath of our shared miracle, serves one and all, its uplifting dynamic seeks a corresponding energy generated by continuous actions to achieve daily goals and fulfillment of purpose, in class and out.

Whatever gifts life into sentient beings is "big bang" energy of unimaginably superior intelligence and creative possibilities, but the gift can only lift those who are lifting themselves.

Spirit and self-discipline are cornerstones of an effective holistic student peer mentoring program. Draw spirit into a mentoring program and it will heighten your mentees' interest in being self-disciplined. This will facilitate the sharpening of academic tools needed for success at college.

Create an inspiring, inspirited environment, a positive field for achievement, and the impetus for self-discipline will follow.

Program managers and mentors, develop relationships with your mentees that will allow them to feel safe enough and courageous enough to dig down deep, reach past their fears, their excuses, their reasons why they can't excel, and find reasons why they *can*, *must*, and *will* achieve their goals. Help shift their self-perceptions from self-doubt to self-empowerment by training them to believe in themselves, day after day, until they come to expect success. Consistently affirm your mentees and self-belief will follow.

Help them tune in to their thoughts, emotions, needs, and actions. Help guide them so they will avoid stumbling over veiled distractions of unmet needs that sap energy and drive. Many of these needs surface for the first time when students find themselves alone at college, responsible for taking care of themselves without on-location support and direction from parents.

Which unmet needs, if met, would allow a mentee to work more effectively on schoolwork? Abraham Maslow wrote about physiological needs (food, water, and shelter), safety needs (security; structure; freedom from fear, anxiety, and chaos), belonging/love needs (family, friends, and affection), esteem needs (self-respect, self-esteem, and achievement), and self-actualization needs (fulfillment of abilities, talents, and self) (199).

MEETING NEEDS EXPRESSED AND UNEXPRESSED

When a student's highest-good needs are met, the student is better able to find the centered calm within, the eye of the human storm, the ideal environment for academic success. If a student's unmet needs are not highest-good—for example, the need to control others, humiliate others, or self-aggrandize at another's expense—these needs are best noted and not acted upon.

Mentoring should be sensitive to the private nature of a mentee's needs, met and unmet, but if a mentee is open to exploring and doing something about his highest-good unmet needs, proceed, with confidentiality respected.

As mentors, be supportive of yourself and your mentees in tone of voice and body language as well as words spoken. Respond not just to what is being said, but how it is said, and, when invited, discuss non-academic needs. But only when invited.

And don't despair—there will be times when you will not be able to draw upon experiences you have had that correspond on some emotional level with the experiences described by your mentees. Remember, you don't have to have had the emotion expressed to be empathetic toward their lives and the needs they have.

To resonate empathetically and authentically, draw upon spirit through its subtle channels: humility, compassion, generosity, truth, love, and joy. Be these traits when mentoring even the most extreme mentee situation and you will be a successful mentor.

BY INVITATION

Some years ago I was director of Mountain View, an accredited school for patients on the adolescent psychiatric unit of St. Vincent Hospital in Santa Fe. I well understood the boundary of having to be invited by a patient/student to discuss non-academic needs that were affecting schoolwork. By mentoring these students with respect, non-judgment, authenticity, empathy, and compassion, while keeping an awareness of professional boundaries, I increased the number of spoken and unspoken invitations I received.

I teach my mentors that they have to be invited in and respectful, always respectful.

THE POWER WITHIN

Mentoring Human Potential pays tribute to all meanings for spirit that brighten a student's life, whether the spiritual dimension is envisioned as a higher power, a survival/ego instinct, or enlightened personal qualities. Regardless, the power within inspires energy and commitment needed to achieve goals that create success.

Program supervisors and mentors enlivened by this energy will inspire similar energy in their mentees, energy that can awaken motivation, enthusiasm, and self-management. But remember—though you can inspire your mentees, their success or lack of success rests on their own shoulders. It is necessary for them to put their shoulders to the wheel, day after day, month after month.

For students who believe in the cosmic resonance and expression of a higher power, mentoring is an opportunity to become one with the higher power's guiding energy and influence. This peaceable frequency is compatible with alpha waves emanating from human brains, and with human joy.

Achieving this peaceable frequency—harmony—in life is not an impossible dream. Students can attain it. All it takes is a shift in consciousness to an everyday perspective that celebrates and partners with the ebullient life force. When fully experienced, spirit infuses every moment with purpose and meaning, two essential resources in any mentor/mentee relationship. *E pluribus unum*—"out of many, one."

For students who don't believe in a higher power, spirit is no less present as a powerful, vibrant energy, activated by the survival demands of living on earth. Spirit can move a student from "I'll do it later," to "I'll do it now."

Regardless of a student's belief or non-belief, being as still as the space between his in and out breath heals the core of all distress. A quiet mind allows for the calming influence of that which does not arise and pass away, an experience of the highest good manifesting within any situation, including academic life.

Embodying the illuminating human spirit helps students achieve what they dream or desire. The process can be remarkably simple. For mentees, spirituality can be introduced in an unaffiliated way—as an aggregate of spiritual qualities. Spirit is as spirit does.

In his book, *Ethics for the New Millennium*, the Dalai Lama wrote: "Spirituality I take to be concerned with the human spirit—such as love and compassion, patience, tolerance, forgiveness, contentment, a sense of harmony—which brings happiness to both self and others" (22).

Be expressions of and guides for these spiritual qualities and the mentoring program will be a transformational experience for you and your mentees. These qualities create positive energy, which supports self-esteem and self-confidence, conduits for academic success.

Human spirit, the aliveness within, is a powerful motivator that generates drive and interest needed to do every task with dedication and heart. Mentors can help mentees discover and draw upon their unique understanding and experience of spirit, *their* spirit, to help motivate them to do what is required when it is required.

SPIRIT OF ST. LOUIS

Are there constraints in American culture regarding spirit? I recently talked to a friend who told me that she and her husband were moving to a large city to start a business that will bring spirituality to corporations. "Of course," she said, "we won't call it spirituality or talk about it directly. We'll disguise all that with communication terms."

I was mystified. When did spirit go underground? Here in America, spirit is as American as apple pie. We name our planes, our teams, our kids—even our dogs—"Spirit" with great affection and understanding. We talk about the "spirit of the law," and "school spirit." It's a beautiful concept. We recognize it as a positive tool—the very thing that makes us the innovative nation we are—"team spirit" and "the spirit to achieve our dreams."

In general, though, academic and business institutions promote a success-oriented but spirit-free approach to learning and making money. At most colleges and high schools it would be unusual for a student peer mentoring program to deliberately emanate from and with spirit.

We as a nation take seriously our Constitution's separation of church and state, especially in our educational institutions. But does that separation include spirit?

As mentors and mentees used my program's everyday practices for stilling and focusing their minds, many of them talked about how they benefited from drawing on a strength they once knew or never knew they had within themselves. This did not come from me. It came from them. Spirit, or lack of spirit, became obvious.

My mentors would come to me and say their mentees were either joyful or not, directed or distressed, or not. They either had the energy for their goals or they didn't. And if they did, and they were successful, they talked about how they had found the strength within to work hard and succeed. They didn't know the strength they summoned was their own spirit but it was, and so over the years my mentoring program evolved quite naturally toward that which turns space into time. Spirit moved into equal partnership with mind and body.

Though successful from its inception, the program's ability to help motivate students increased as spirit came into balance with mind and body.

In remarks made when he received the Templeton Prize for the advancement and research of spiritual matters, Charles Taylor said, "The deafness of many philosophers, social scientists and historians to the spiritual dimension can be remarkable." Taylor suggested this was damaging because it "affects the culture of the media and educated public opinion in general."

IN ALIGNMENT WITH SPIRIT

Everyone has different sensibilities, as personal as a fingerprint. I would not presume, nor should any mentor presume to intrude upon the personal style of our mentees. This is not about ego or style. It is about graduating, plain and simple. Graduation is the overarching goal. Through the inspiring success of graduation, students can taste the fruits of that which deepens the mystery.

How does one align one's self with spirit? I recall Dr. Keeney's comment: "When mentor and mentee submit themselves in an open and good way to being moved by a mind greater than their psychological selves, spirit takes notice and enters the scene."

Dr. Keeney suggests a way of being in the world that accesses the high energy and guidance of spirit. There are activities that do the same, awakening and harnessing the power within. There are peaceful touchstones which quiet thoughts, inducing the alpha state, e.g., meditation, yoga, deep breathing and exercising, listening to music, playing with one's pets, reading, chanting, prayer, mindful walking or running, even staring at an aquarium.

There are countless paths to spirit. For some it's a walk through wildflowers, the stars at night, or sitting on a river bank. For others, spirit is experienced in a church, synagogue, temple, mosque, or a kiva. Our paths are many—greater in number than those walking their path.

Is our mainstream culture ill at ease with actions that engender humility and reverence while quieting the mind? The question is worth considering. A mind at peace with itself neutralizes, slows, or stops the distracting chatter of inner dialogue, self-judgments, and judgments of others. When the chatter becomes indistinct or muted, spirit expands into the moment with great energy and purpose, whether activated by a higher power or the brilliance of the human spirit allowed to flourish.

However defined, alignment with spirit should be a goal each week for your mentees and for yourself. When approached harmoniously, spirit embraces all paths to itself.

THE BREATH OF RELIEF

The close relationship of breath to spirit was understood long ago. The origin of the English word soul is a word that meant breath or wind. The Latin *spiritus*, spirit, synonymous with soul, originally meant "breath."

Breathing exercises are a recommended method for drawing forth that which is the antithesis of self-consciousness, higher power or not. A breathing exercise can be done anywhere and is especially helpful in the minutes before beginning an exam. It helps relieve stress and calms the practitioner's mind, allowing for greater sustained attention and insight.

This is important because motivation and action to achieve goals occur through insight into why, for example, it is more important to study than party. Breathing exercises quiet the mind and foster insights that can help reveal what is required.

CREATING PEACEFUL LIVES IN VIOLENT TIMES

While spirit's positive energy embraces all paths to itself, we live in a world where the grace of positive energy co-exists with its polar opposite—violence. For many, the fury of each day's global turmoil filters through TVs and newspapers, modeling aggression as a societally-approved way to handle conflict. Video games are recreational testament to this reality. Our human tendency toward violence and cruelty is consistently exploited as entertainment by mass media, deeply affecting our daily life.

Students may falter academically because of cruel or callous comments tossed their way in a dorm, cafeteria, student union, or bar—just about anywhere. Academically-focused minds may become distracted by the difficulty of trying to fit in to a culture alienated from its need for peace, love, and understanding.

I don't think it is an over-statement to assert that, with noteworthy exceptions, mass media condition students from an early age to use socially accepted forms of aggression as tools for conflict resolution. The most commonly accepted form is gossip.

During their high school years, many first-year college students feared the sting of gossip and put-downs by peers. For many, the everyday possibility of being ridiculed or socially rejected was an educational subtext that currently may be contributing to their psychological makeup.

When I make a check of any day's media and sit down to watch the six o'clock news, the global grip of humankind's violent tendencies is apparent and the role it has on the balance or imbalance of partying to studying and the academic performance of students is worth considering.

Regardless of how lovingly or wisely parents raise or do not raise their kids, our shock-and-sell culture is often their greatest influence.

A SAFE PLACE

Student peer mentoring offers a much-needed way to authentically and confidentially discuss how a mentee is really doing, without fear of personal vulnerability. Mentoring with spirit can raise a mentee's self-esteem that might otherwise be undermined by socially and academically competitive college life.

My peer mentors celebrate spirit as they mentor. They imbue restorative energy, achieved through harmonious balance of mind, body, and spirit. This uplifting energy reverberates throughout the mentoring program as a self-renewing resource.

WHEN THE ROAD UNWINDS

To know the road ahead, listen to those coming back.—Yang Li An

As you think about creating a student peer mentoring program, being a mentor or a mentee, consider the path, your path, which has led you to this moment. Here are tracings of my own path.

It's a hot mid-August. My parents drop me off at American University in Washington, DC and we wave goodbye as they drive away. I don't know a soul at American but everyone thinks I'm going to be just fine. I did well in high school, so I must have the skills and knowledge to succeed, right? Little did I know.

I actually arrived without knowledge of how to study and learn well. I had a sense of inevitability about starting college. I was seventeen. I thought I knew everything. I had the commonly held attitude of many first-year students in private colleges: "What else am I going to do after high school?" It never occurred to me not to go to college. I certainly didn't have the gratitude I would have now for the opportunity to get a college education.

I had a rough first semester, completely taken by surprise that I missed my family and friends in Croton-on-Hudson, New York as much as I did. First semester I had no one at American to turn to and I held on white-knuckled until Spring semester. I struggled to pay attention in class, too lonely and distracted by my unmet emotional needs to do well academically, all the while trying to hide it.

The support I needed wasn't there. I didn't have tutors or study groups. I didn't know what to expect on exams. I didn't have a mentor. I would have been greatly helped by a peer mentoring program during my first semester at American University, even though I wasn't on academic probation. I would have benefited from the guidance of an upper class student who knew the academic and social ropes of my university.

Enter Mrs. Yarnell, my own guiding light and mentor. Shirley Yarnell—the seldom celebrated, committed, and gifted teacher that steps forward, the one teacher everyone remembers who makes a difference in their life. Thank you, Madam, from the bottom of my heart. What you saw in me I was able to see in myself and by the end of the semester I was doing well academically and socially.

DESERT EPIPHANY

It's a hot mid-August, many years later. I'm walking through an arroyo, ten miles from where I live in Santa Fe, New Mexico. As I move through the high desert, I think about the students on academic probation with whom I work at the College of Santa Fe. Brave and vulnerable, they face the same challenges I did at their age, many without any of the advantages and privileges I had. If I had a problem getting through my first semester, I can only imagine how much more difficult it must be for many of them.

At that moment, my life's work takes on another commitment: creating and supervising a student peer mentoring program at the College of Santa Fe and training supervisors to set up mentoring programs at other educational institutions.

Who better than a peer to inspire, teach, guide, and model successful study and learning habits? No one knows the challenges and struggles of being a student better than a fellow student who can mentor as an insider. Mentors can help orient and stabilize mentees' college lives, as one would have for me that first semester my parents waved goodbye.

This August day I imagine student peer mentoring programs that would be holistic, addressing academic, social, and spiritual aspects of living successfully. A holistic approach would recognize and engage the needs of mentors and mentees as multi-dimensional beings with complex inner lives. Nothing to it but to do it, so I did it.

CHAPTER TWO

Create a Student Peer Mentoring Program

Once you have decided to create a student peer mentoring program, you need to get a commitment and funds from your educational institution. The process can be an uncomplicated one. Here is the straightforward proposal I sent to the college vice president of academic and student affairs.

PROPOSAL FOR A STUDENT PEER MENTORING PROGRAM FOR STUDENTS ON ACADEMIC PROBATION

"The need is clear. Our students on academic probation require additional help to strengthen their academic weaknesses so they can succeed in college. A Student Peer Mentoring Program would strengthen their academic skills and help them adjust to the challenges of college life, leveling the academic playing field for them.

To help our academic probation students and aid the college's desire to retain as high a percentage of students as possible, I propose a Student Peer Mentoring Program. As a condition for admission to the college, academic probation students would be required to be part of the college's mentoring program.

To start, I would train five student peer mentors who would be assigned an average of three mentees, all first-year students on academic probation. Mentors would meet with their mentees once a week for an hour, and once a week with me for a half hour. Once a month I would meet with mentors as a group for an hour.

The philosophical approach of the mentoring program would be holistic, conveyed through a comprehensive four-hour training session required for peer mentors. As the program's supervisor, I would meet with or phone mentees during the semester. The program would be evaluated each semester by peer mentors and mentees."

Within weeks, the vice president approved my proposal and asked for a budget. Days later I sent one and it, too, was approved.

In keeping with my policy of protecting the financial aspects of my work with institutions and private clients with whom I consult, mentor or coach, I offer a sample budget as a model for the reader.

STUDENT PEER MENTORING PROGRAM BUDGET

This budget (to be adjusted for more or fewer mentees) includes a four-hour peer mentor training, training materials, three-ring binders, weekly mentor/mentee meetings, weekly one-on-one meetings between mentors and me, and a once a month group mentor meeting.

Training:
5 students for 4 hours $200.00

Mentors' weekly meetings with mentees:
5 mentors x 3 mentees each x 1 hour per week x 32 weeks $4,800.00

Mentors' weekly meetings with program supervisor and prep time:
5 mentors x 32 weeks x 1 hour per week $1,600.00

Training Materials:
(Includes 5 copies of *Becoming a Master Student*) $450.00
Total: **$7,050.00**

Mentors receive $10.00/hour
Returning mentors receive $10.50/hour

Colleges that don't have funding for a student peer mentoring program, or that prefer a non-monetary involvement of mentors, can consider giving college credit for each semester completed as mentor. Credit may also be considered for mentees as well.

FOCUS QUESTIONS

Who are your mentees?

Many of us, at various times in our lives, need someone to be our North Star, if only for a while. Mentees are everyone's sons and daughters, the girl next door, the boy down the street. They are you when you need a leg up.

Mentees may be on academic probation, or not, depending on the mentoring program. The program I set up at the College of Santa Fe was for students who were on academic probation, with exceptions. Either way, mentors will have far more in common with their mentees than differences. They will share the same human condition, filled with similar dreams and fears.

Mentees are often students who never learned and practiced academic and social skills that are the tools for success. For all students, these tools are survival skills. Regardless of aptitudes and academic concentrations, all students are in school to learn how to survive and thrive in our twenty-first century world, which has made everyone's life high-risk.

"Survival through Strengths" was the theme of a workshop I gave at a Teaching Academic Survival Skills conference in West Palm Beach, Florida. My presentation, "Supporting High Risk Students with Departmental Peer Mentoring," asserted that student peer mentoring programs were unmatched as a way to develop strength-based survival skills in mentees and their mentors, survival skills that lead to graduation and success in life after college. Workshop participants shared stories about how their survival skills led to their success as educators. Everyone had stories.

We all need well-developed survival skills to successfully meet the globally competitive character of our century. Mentees may have to play catch up, and may have greater need for a human compass, a mentor, to illumine their way for a while.

Who are your mentees? What are their challenges? First-year academic probation students face the same challenges every new college student faces, and then some. None can be sure of the answer to the question, "Will I be able to handle the academic demands of college?"

Academic probation students also struggle with the knowledge that they will probably have to devote more time to schoolwork than other students if they are going to succeed. They may not want to share this truth with potential friends. In fact, some under-prepared students may respond to their need to study more and work harder by socializing more and partying harder.

All first-year students also have the daunting task of discovering who they can trust in their new environment. Everyone has a good first act. Among the judgments made (consciously or subconsciously) after each first impression is whether the latest person met can be trusted. The usual conclusion? "It's too soon to know."

First-year students realize that friendships can only be relied on after mutual loyalty and sacrifice have been shown and it's too early in the semester for that to have happened. This reality conflicts with the need to have a trusted friend with whom to share the difficulties of starting college life. The result may be uncertainty and anxiety as students search for the emotional comfort and college life that new friends can provide.

Putting on a game face, most newly-arrived students try to generate social acceptance by beginning their college life with a ready smile and social projections of what is most likable in themselves.

Establishing a college social community takes longer than establishing an academic community. Students quickly learn the rules and requirements of classroom behavior and academic grading. The rules and requirements of social life take longer to establish because the range of possible behavior is considerably greater. Social boundaries shift from group to group as students try to find classmates with similar interests, personalities, and habits.

Especially during the first few months of the semester, attempts by students to be liked and fit in result in varying degrees of acceptance, rejection, and mood swings, ranging from having the time of their lives, to being depressed and motivationally flat-lined. Students who spiral downward (some on academic probation) often hide their despair, unwilling to further alienate themselves by sharing with peers the depth of their unease.

First semester is a series of first impressions and most students feel that "I'm lonely and depressed" isn't a good first impression. Dorm and classroom meet-and-greets require a winning persona, regardless of how a student is really feeling. This can result in surface acceptance by peers and a concurrent aloneness and disconnect from college life, with undesirable consequences.

Students may camouflage unsettled psychological states by wearing invisible introductory social masks. Sunny "How you doing?" smiles may conceal less sunny emotions: loneliness, homesickness, and instability. An academic probation student may be among those who have difficulty establishing a successful college identity with a group of unknown peers who cannot, for some time at least, replace family and friends back home. The implications for academic success may be significant—untended, unshared emotional needs may manifest as an inability to focus meaningfully on schoolwork.

How do you select mentees?

Which students are best suited to be mentees? What, if any, should be their conditions for enrollment?

Any student assigned to the Student Peer Mentoring Program, whether on academic probation or considered to be at high risk for probation, receives a letter from the college's vice president of academic and student affairs outlining the terms of their enrollment, which include mandatory participation in the Student Peer Mentoring Program.

I've run the program where participation was required, and where it was optional. What works best, I have found, is mandatory participation of incoming students on academic probation, with consequences if they miss more than two meetings with their mentors. I am the administrator to whom mentees are referred if they miss two mentoring meetings without extenuating circumstances, though mentors have the discretion to allow more than two missed meetings if they think it warranted.

When the program is mandatory, I send the following letter to each student on academic probation:

Dear _____,

I hope this letter finds you well and enjoying the summer. As noted in your conditional acceptance to the college on academic probation, you will be participating as a "mentee" in the Fall semester Student Peer Mentoring Program. Mentees are students guided to academic success by their mentors, well-trained upper division classmates.

The mentoring program has helped many students get off academic probation and achieve scholastic success. It can do the same for you.

Here is some information about the Student Peer Mentoring Program that will give you a sense of what you can expect from the program and what the program will expect from you:

- Mentees meet once a week for an hour with their mentor at an agreed upon time and place, often the library. Confidentiality is guaranteed.
- To help you and your mentor understand how you study and learn, soon after you meet, your mentor will give you a Learning and Study Strategies Inventory. This inventory will help identify areas of your knowledge, skills, motivation, and attitude that you may need to improve. These are areas you can expect your mentor to help you develop during the semester. In addition, your mentor will help you stay on task with your schoolwork, will guide you to resources and help with any problems that may arise, in class or out.
- Each week, you and your mentor will co-create a Seven-Day Plan. This plan is a commitment you will make, primarily with yourself, to identify and work hard to achieve your goals. The program's approach is holistic (mind, body, and spirit), seeking to optimize these aspects of everyday life so you will achieve your primary goal—graduation.
- At least once during the semester, either by phone or in person, you and I will discuss the mentoring program and whether it is helping you achieve your goals.
- Your mentor will be dedicated to your success at the college and will expect that you will be equally dedicated. While we want you to have a relaxed, personal relationship with your mentor, we're serious about our shared goal—to help you get off academic probation and become a successful, independent learner. Should you miss more than two meetings with your mentor, you will be asked to meet with me to discuss your absences.
- During your first week at the college, your mentor will phone you and set up a meeting time and place. Should you have any questions about the mentoring program, call me at (505) 466-2878.

On the back of this letter, please provide the following information:

Name:

Cell phone:

Email:

Major:

Preference for mentor:
Male ___ Female ___ No preference ___

- How can the mentoring program help you succeed?
- What caused your academic problems in the past?
- Are your learning and study skills up to the challenges of college life?
- Do personal problems affect your ability to succeed academically?

Please return this letter in the enclosed, prepaid envelope.

With best wishes for a successful semester,

Scott Seldin
Program Manager for Peer Mentoring
College of Santa Fe

Who are your mentors?
They are any of us whose lives have fallen into place and who are now able to help others do what we ourselves can do. They are everyone's sons and daughters, the girl next door, the boy down the street. They are great communicators, leaders with generosity of spirit. They are authentic, empathetic, and some of them are yesterday's mentees. They are motivating, supportive, "go-to" students who receive reward from mentoring, regardless of whether or not they are paid. They take pleasure in holding the light for others.

How do you select mentors and match them with mentees?
Many of the mentors I select are recommended by faculty who respond to an email I send, describing the Student Peer Mentoring Program and asking for names of students they think would make great mentors. My

email informs that recommended students should have a GPA of at least 3.0, with occasional exceptions.

I phone recommended prospective mentors, describe the program, and ask if they're interested in interviewing for a mentor position.

The day I send the email to faculty, I place a flyer by the entrance to the college cafeteria:

YOU CAN MAKE A DIFFERENCE!

Be part of a team of mentors who are making a difference in the lives of their fellow students, their mentees. I am interviewing for paid mentor positions. Are you interested?

To qualify, you must be an excellent student, able to motivate, teach learning and study strategies, and guide three students to success.

For an interview, call Scott Seldin, Program Manager for Peer Mentoring, at (505) 466-2878.

My interviews are informal, conversational, held in my office. I want to know if the candidates are friendly. Are they emotionally accessible? Good communicators? Empathetic? Engaging? Someone I would want to mentor me if I was a college student who needed a mentor? Are they eager to be mentors? What are their academic strengths and weaknesses? How do they motivate themselves? What qualities do they have that would make them great mentors?

If it doesn't conflict with a mentee's indicated gender preference for a mentor, I match mentors with mentees who are in the same academic department.

Henry James might have been among the first to refer to the laws of attraction when he said, "People like people who are like themselves. Effective communicators instinctively know how to 'match' the physiology, energy and voice tone and tempo of the individual that they are speaking with in ways that are natural and congruent."

CHAPTER THREE

Mentor Workshop Training

A HOLISTIC APPROACH THROUGH SPIRIT AND SELF-DISCIPLINE

The Sunday afternoon before the semester's first day of classes, I give my mentor training. The current iteration is a workshop training, structured to draw mentors personally into the dynamic of living and mentoring with holistic awareness: mind, body, and spirit.

Spirit is part of all aspects of my training, present without trumpeting its presence. "Chop wood, carry water"—I keep it simple. Spirit and self-discipline are foundational.

The seven mentors in my mentoring program were carefully chosen the previous spring. Three are returning as mentors after mentoring successfully last year. Two have worked as tutors for the Academic Resource Center; each has a reputation at the college for being highly responsible, academically successful, effective, and likable communicators with their peers and teachers.

When we gather in August, the atmosphere is informal and friendly. We sit around a large table and my training begins.

Note: what follows in chapters three through seven is the model I use to create a student peer mentoring program. I have added to my training a reconstruction of its tone, pacing, and character. When I created this workshop training, I imagined I was talking to a small group of students in a comfortable living room, students who would be the heart and soul of my Student Peer Mentoring Program. I invite you to imagine taking a seat with the mentors in training.

Program supervisors, present or future, I encourage you to adapt my training to suit the needs of your students. And mentors, use this training model to develop your own voice and style.

THE MENTOR WORKSHOP TRAINING BEGINS

In the interest of equality consciousness, herein, gender references that don't refer to a specific person will alternate from chapter to chapter, when these references appear in a chapter.

"Welcome to my workshop training for mentors of the college Student Peer Mentoring Program. This is an interactive workshop that will bring you personally into the mentoring program. We're all in the program, myself included. The pads on the table in front of you have an outline of this workshop, with activities you will be participating in this afternoon.

So, we're going to begin at the beginning—the workshop's introduction."

Activity: Participants will briefly introduce themselves to the group.

Discussion: Share a mentor in your lives who made a difference. What was it about your mentor that affected you so deeply?

"Thank you for being mentors. Each of you is going to make an important difference in the lives of your mentees. In fact, you may be the reason a mentee is successful enough to stay at the college. You have been hired because you are well qualified, successful students, able to achieve high GPAs while enjoying active social lives.

You are all effective communicators with good learning and study skills. Your personalities are upbeat and naturally suited for the work you will be doing. That said, mentoring is going to challenge you and reveal your own strengths and weaknesses, as well as those of your mentees. It will challenge your assumptions about how your peers should act as students and classmates.

To be a successful mentor, accept your mentees the way they are while helping them set goals each week, inspired to achieve their potential. Mentoring is going to test your patience and, quite possibly, your ego's need to see results quickly. To be a good mentor you will need a sense of humor and a compassionate understanding of the human condition.

I have developed a mentoring program that should be tailored to the academic needs of each of your mentees—a program that is enjoyable and makes them feel worthy. This requires authentic, trusting relationships so that mentees can feel safe enough to reflect on their deeper truths. Buried dreams and the damage done by prior school humiliations and boredom may have turned them off to education and teachers in general.

Mentoring from the heart builds trust more quickly than any other mentoring perspective. If trust is slow to come, continue to mentor from the heart. Be patient. Trust is personal. If a mentee is invited into the inner world of her mentor, however briefly, she is more likely to invite her mentor into her own inner world where obstacles to success can be directly and gently engaged. This is where habits that sabotage can be changed into habits that facilitate success.

Of course, the trust that allows for sharing inner lives can't be rushed. It must be both earned and desired, though in rare instances it happens upon meeting. If a mentee is uncomfortable talking from a personal perspective, talk from a perspective she feels comfortable sharing. And when you do share your own inner world as mentor, keep it brief. If you spend more than five minutes talking about yourself, you may be indulging your need to be the center of attention. Think of the mentors you've had over the years. My guess is you never felt they were egotistical in their relationship with you."

Discussion: Our thoughts, expectations, and concerns about mentoring.

"Mentoring is a shared journey and a shared gift. As memorable as your most memorable mentor is, you have an opportunity to be that memorable in someone's life and heart."

THE BAR OF POTENTIAL GENTLY RAISED

"I want your work to be important to you. I want you to be personally involved in your job. Use your academic strengths, your ability to communicate well, your positive, likable personalities to connect with your mentees. You have been chosen because you have what it takes to be exceptionally good peer mentors. Use your experiences as students and your knowledge of how things work around here. I hope you will take your work in the Student Peer Mentoring Program as seriously as I do.

Sometimes being on academic probation will motivate a mentee to work hard. Sometimes it will demoralize her and affect her ability to concentrate for very long on schoolwork. It is difficult to sustain a feeling of equanimity when you know your admission to the college is conditional.

Freshmen on academic probation must participate in our Student Peer Mentoring Program and get grade point averages of 2.0 or better. Our goal, for mentees who want it, is for them to get off academic probation with a grade point average of 3.0 or better. If this is unrealistic, ask your mentees to set their academic bar as high as possible while maintaining a good chance of success.

If a mentee psychologically and academically defines herself by her academic probation status, talk about past accomplishments. When did she last accomplish her goals and what motivated her then to succeed? If a mentee has succeeded once, she can succeed again. Just as conditions for failure may have come together in a past academic context, changed habits and heightened motivation can create conditions for success.

Discuss the conditions your mentees need at the college to achieve their goals, for example, when and where they are going to study and what habits or temptations might get in the way of achieving their goals.

How can mentors inspire mentees to overcome the inclination to avoid unpleasurable academic assignments? By highlighting their pleasurable accomplishments. That's why we co-establish achievable goals for mentees each week. When they accomplish their goals, their confidence builds and they experience the pleasure of achievement. Greater confidence and motivation lead to greater academic success.

Your job as mentor is to encourage your mentees to take the actions needed each day to create holistic success: mind, body, and spirit. This will probably require you to change your mentees' perceptions of what is possible for them. But keep in mind, good mentoring offers suggestions without being prescriptive. Illuminate the way without becoming the way.

For many of your mentees, your up-close support and belief in them week after week will be a first. They may resist improving bad study or learning habits because the pressure to maintain improved habits may make them uneasy. That's why it is important to establish a personal relationship with each mentee. They certainly don't want a stranger telling them about the academic habits they should improve."

THE MENTOR/MENTEE RELATIONSHIP

"At the heart of every mentor/mentee relationship is a basic question. As the caterpillar asked Alice, 'Who are you?'

The answer to this question should be ever revealing itself through your relationships with each of your mentees. When mentor and mentee meet, ideally they will have mutually agreeable chemistry, which will hasten trust and a deepening answer to the caterpillar's question."

> **Activity:** Have mentors pair off and sit opposite each other for a ten to fifteen-minute role playing exercise. They will take turns being mentees and mentors. As mentees, each will present a difficult, fictional academic and/or social situation to their mentor who will respond and initiate discussion.

"What did you learn from this exercise? How do you feel when you're talking to someone with academic problems? Do you relate differently to students who have worse grades than you? Better grades? Are you aware of what you may be subconsciously projecting?

Keep it simple when you first meet your mentees. Get to know them the way you would a first-year roommate, a stranger with whom you share a situation. Be open, regardless of how open they seem toward you. It may take them time to respond in a personal way, but you will have set precedent. Share backgrounds, likes, dislikes, majors, hobbies, and why you're at the college.

Building trust starts with this baseline: *under no circumstances are you ever to divulge any aspect of your mentoring meetings with anyone*. Not with your boyfriend, your girlfriend, your roommate, your best friend, your parents—not with anyone but me, as the program's supervisor. Deserved trust means *complete privacy*. Start developing trust with a signed agreement to keep all mentoring discussions absolutely private. This is an unshakable cornerstone of the mentoring program. Any mentor violating it will be discharged immediately. Trust me, I've done it. Fortunately, I've only had to do it once.

Authenticity and trust are essential qualities for a successful mentor/mentee relationship. These qualities can't be faked or established on demand. They have to be a natural development in a relationship that is true to itself. This is not easily done. Most people are slow to trust, having learned about our species from experience. Mentors should be obvious exceptions to an understandable everyday wariness toward humans.

How do you, as mentors, develop the trust with your mentees that is necessary for our program to achieve its potential? By being trustworthy. We can understand trustworthiness by reflecting on the characteristics of people we trust: those who tell the truth and are honest; who listen in a personal, confidential way; who come through for us in good times and bad; who always have our best interest at heart; who take pleasure in our successes and have understanding and encouragement for our setbacks. Sometimes it's not what is said that's important, it's the feeling that passes across the table.

Ideally, each of your mentor/mentee relationships will develop mutual trust. Your mentees will trust that you take a personal interest in them, have the ability to help, and will never humiliate or betray them. You will trust that your mentees will show up on time for meetings, and if unable to make a meeting, will call in advance to explain and reschedule.

How you, as mentors, come across to your mentees is very important. Establish authentic rapport. Be someone you would like if you were your own mentor. Be present, actively in the moment, personally interested in them and committed to their well-being. If they have to spend time responding to a detached or self-absorbed mentor, they probably need a different mentor.

Your positive energy, personal interest, and belief in them will help them find the same in themselves. Motivate by being motivated. Generate enthusiasm for your time together. Turn your meetings into a process of self-discovery, self-motivation, and setting timelines for achieving the daily goals of their next seven days.

Equality is important for trust to develop in the mentor/mentee relationship and therefore the psychological obstacles to equality are worth noting. A mentee may feel embarrassed to need mentoring and may withdraw her interest, feeling that the very nature of the relationship places her in an inferior position. The mentor may indeed have a subtle sense of superiority over the mentee. After all, she's the guide, not the guided.

In truth, any sense of superiority is an illusion. We live in communities where we all depend on each other for our survival. Unfortunately, many people, striving for ego-satisfaction, believe the life they are living is not dependent on others. In our 'survival of the fittest' society, with its ethos of self-reliance and rugged individualism, receiving help from others is often interpreted as weakness. Perhaps, in addition to celebrating Independence Day, we should celebrate Interdependence Day, where we recognize and honor those who are helping us and those we are helping.

Mentors should be keenly aware of all who have reached out to them with a helping hand and should dispel any perceived sense of inequality by embodying equality as a way of being and relating.

Can equality be maintained when the mentee is more obviously accountable to the mentor? It can if mentors are perceived by mentees as simply carrying out the requirements of the program, rather than asserting power. Accountability should not diminish the mentor/mentee sense of equality. It is important for the mentor to remember that the mentor/mentee relationship is one of peers.

What if it is clear from the start that the chemistry is bad between mentor and mentee? Speak with me as soon as possible. Perhaps another mentor is having the same problem and these mentors and mentees could switch. A bad mentor/mentee match should be handled sensitively, with care taken to avoid anyone feeling a sense of personal failure.

When invited to do so, one way the mentor/mentee relationship is enriched is through discussions about social life at the college. While the primary purpose of the mentor/mentee relationship is to help the mentee succeed academically, don't underestimate the positive impact a well-balanced social life can have on academic achievement.

A mentor can help accomplish this by making social life a potential subject for discussion during part of each meeting. Talk about how you developed your social life at the college, with dorm life, activities, clubs, and other ideas that will help a mentee socially.

Another area of college life that will contribute to bonding between mentors and mentees is professors. Chances are a mentor has taken classes with some of her mentee's teachers or knows through the grapevine their reputations, requirements, and teaching styles. A mentor must walk a tight line, though, careful not to malign the reputation of a teacher.

Mentor/mentee relationships will inspire and be most successful when allowed to develop in a natural, unforced way. Keep it fresh and 'in the moment.' Keep it positive and welcoming. To develop ideal mentor/mentee relationships, listen to your mentees from a place of small ego. Mentor with a quiet, still mind—ideal for deep listening—where words are heard with ears and heart. Discuss active, deep listening with your mentees as an important practice, socially and in classrooms. Develop this practice when you meet with your mentees.

The tone of your meetings should be friendly and caring, not intrusive or parental. Find out how things are going for them and briefly share how things are going for you. Of course, a mentee doesn't have to talk about her social life but it helps to know how that aspect of her life is going.

Ask if she had any problems or frustrations during the week that she would like to talk about. If your opinions are requested, give them. If not, don't. How do you know if your opinions are requested? Just ask.

Dr. Rey Carr, CEO of Peer Resources, Inc., Victoria, BC, Canada, suggests: 'Help mentors learn that discussion of social life is an acceptable topic but only within the context of its impact on academic success. In other words the mentor is asking, *How is your social life affecting your study time?* The mentor isn't interested in specific details about social life (i.e., who are you dating? etc.) but how social life and academic life are mixing.'

Mentors, your challenge is to develop each of your mentee relationships so the relationship itself supports your mentoring. The mentor/mentee relationship should be easy on the psyche—enjoyable, supportive, and productive. You don't have to be great friends with your mentees. The relationship can work very well if you guide them to a balanced, harmonious, and holistically successful life without being a personal part of it.

Can accountability turn the relationship into one where the mentee resents being accountable? Easily, if it turns into a power relationship. The mentoring field should always be level.

Develop relationships that are as connected as possible without sacrificing the potential to academically and psychologically prepare each mentee to achieve their goals for the next seven days.

Be aware of what you are projecting. You don't want a mentee looking at you and seeing one of her parents looking back. This can create resistance to being mentored, which may cause the mentee to stop working collaboratively with her mentor.

The conditioning of most teenagers to any authority figure is reactive and often quite negative. You can expect your mentees to react negatively if they perceive any hint of a power trip in the guise of 'what's best for them.' For mentee transformation to occur, motivation should come primarily from within rather than without.

Help your mentees discover their sources of motivation but do so discreetly and unobtrusively. Your mentor/mentee relationships should be guided by you, as mentor, co-attentive to what is in their best interest. How can you be sure what that is? You can't, but together you can shape a plan that makes the effort, a plan that decides on the most important priorities for the next seven days.

The questions you ask should elicit responses from mentees that help clarify their most important priorities for the next seven days and inspire them to a greater understanding of their own lives.

Your questions should be open-ended. Avoid the yes/no answers invited by closed questions such as, 'Have you had a good week?' Instead, ask 'How did your week go?' or 'What was it like at the concert?' rather than, 'Did you have a good time at the concert?'

Your questions should draw your mentees into a natural flow of thought and discussion. Mentoring should generate exchanges that lead to reflection, insight, and inspired commitment to achieve goals and enjoy life.

A goal of a mentor's questions is to lead mentees to become their own authorities, overseeing their own lives, rather than looking to others (i.e., parents, teachers, and friends) to exercise control, however obvious or subtle, over their beliefs, behaviors, and parameters of feeling. Mentoring can be considered successful when it leads a mentee to sustained, high-functioning self-management and actualized potential.

Have an awareness of how your energy and personality affect the energy and motivation of your mentees. When a mentee leaves her mentor, she should feel more energized and positive than when she arrived.

If you develop negative feelings toward a mentee, don't project your negativity. Contact me immediately. We'll figure out ways to deal with your feelings while you continue to give your wholehearted, unwavering support. And if that doesn't work, we'll find another mentor for your mentee."

SEVEN SUGGESTIONS

"Mentors, mentees—in fact, everyone can benefit from 'Seven Suggestions for Genuine Dialogue' (adapted by Veterans for Peace, Santa Fe Chapter, from www.tikkun.org). I recommend that mentors and mentees use these suggestions in everyday life, inside and outside the classroom.

'In order to make any kind of change, it is necessary to be able to communicate effectively what you believe. Some may think like you. Some may think differently. But in order to have any kind of exchange—whether one-on-one, to an audience, or in a structured forum, such as a meeting—it is crucial that you engage in dialogue. When talking with people who disagree with you, this can be a challenge. It is difficult to refrain from interrupting or growing angry when you feel certain that the other person is misinformed or misguided. But in your certainty, you may well miss something—and you clearly may miss an opportunity to persuade someone of what you believe. Regardless of the situation, here are a few communication tips:

1. LISTEN ACTIVELY
   Focus on what the person is saying, not your next argument. You can always take some time to think before responding.

2. RESPECT THE OTHER
   This is crucial. Whomever you are talking with must feel respected, or they will not speak honestly and will not be open to your ideas. Respect is signaled by refraining from interrupting or speaking over someone; respect also requires avoiding language that is abusive or accusatory. Speak with someone as you would want to be spoken with. Make the conversation safe.

3. REMAIN CALM
   No one ever changes their opinions because they are intimidated, or when they get furious.

4. ASK QUESTIONS THAT WILL HELP OPEN A PERSON'S MIND
   Research shows that people change their minds NOT when they are listening but when they are speaking, working out what they really think.

5. SPEAK FROM WHAT YOU FEEL
   Express this literally. As opposed to 'You're wrong, and you're being idiotic,' it'll be much more effective to say: 'I feel you're only taking in part of the story. Have you thought about . . . . ?'

6. PICK YOUR BATTLES
    There are some people who will never think differently. Don't waste emotional energy on these situations. Remember that dialogue is like baseball: if you bat .300 you are doing really well.

7. REMAIN CALM
    You'll learn something.'"

INTENTION

"Most students will say, if asked, that their intention is to do well in school. If they believe their intention is good and they give it the old college try, they did what they could, right? Not necessarily. Many students hide behind their belief that their intention is to do well. They can somehow feel OK about themselves if they believe this because even if they don't do the work, they meant to.

Intention is an important consideration when mentoring, but it requires far more deliberately focused energy and personal commitment than 'My intention is to do well.' Intention for individual and collective highest good should be consciously considered at the beginning of each day. This dedicates a student to the day's goals and a way of being in the world that is harmonious.

What are your intentions as a mentor? What are your mentees' intentions? For mentees, establishing intention each day should be associated directly with achieving daily goals of Seven-Day Plans. The more specific the intention established, the more likely that success will follow. It could be said that intention is the mother of achievement.

Know each mentee's intention. Is she willing to commit the time and energy and make the sacrifices necessary to achieve the success she seeks? What percentage of an hour studying out of class does she spend thinking about dinner, a personal problem, or reacting internally to what someone said or didn't say?"

PURPOSE—A POWERFUL MOTIVATOR

"What is your purpose?" The answer to this question, however tentative, can provide powerful motivation for a student to do her best. No shrug-of-the-shoulders answer will do. If a strong sense of personal purpose is to motivate a mentee, purpose should be shaped by deep reflection.

Do humans have a purpose as a species? Do we each have a unique and separate purpose, ever evolving, ever revealing itself to us? It is important to know the why-we-be character of our life force, our spirit, our innermost direction, our most compelling reasons for any actions, be they cosmic, utilitarian, or the universe that stretches between.

Mentors, do you know what values and morality accompany your own purpose? Are you modeling values and expectations on those of your parents? Do your friends live with a sense of purpose? What motivates you today? Why?

Contemplate these questions and understand how mentoring fits in with your own purpose. College is an opportunity to achieve goals that are expressions of a student's deepest, most personal reasons for getting up in the morning. After contemplating your own reasons and steppingstone goals, help your mentees do the same.

There is always an appropriate time to have a discussion about purpose and it will vary from mentee to mentee, depending on their natures, the nature of your relationship with them, and their propensity to reflect philosophically on the meaning of their lives.

Discovering your own and your mentees' overarching life purpose and its day-to-day expression are important because energy, self-managed direction, and persistence flow from knowing your *raison d'etre*. Knowing what you want to do with the life you've been given sparks motivation needed to meet the challenges posed by expected and unexpected daily challenges.

We want our mentees to have self-sustaining motivation so they will stick with their Seven-Day Plans, even when tired or discouraged. We want them to get help when needed, go to classes, and stay current with schoolwork. A sense of purpose makes this possible.

As the poet Mary Oliver wrote, 'Tell me what is it you plan to do with your one wild and precious life?'"

Activity: Have mentors write a Statement of Purpose. Follow with discussion.

"Mentors, share your Statement of Purpose with your mentees and ask that they do the same for you. With personal purpose as a bridge to personal dreams, draw connections between and among all the classes your mentees are taking and the underlying reasons they are enrolled at the college. Spirit is most buoyant when purpose is in alignment with a person's highest good. Discuss what they think is their highest good and whether they are committed to achieving it.

Inspire your mentees to work with discipline and passion in response to their most compelling reasons to do well. You may be motivated to achieve your potential at college because of your love of learning, especially in your major. You may be motivated because you've always been motivated and it's your nature—all well and good and to be hoped for, but your sources of motivation may be quite different from those of your mentees. They may be in college and motivated because they equate wealth with success and the only way to be successful is with a college degree.

Your mentees' sources for motivation may be antithetical to your belief system and you may be personally turned off by their reasons for being in college. Turn yourself back on. Honor them by supporting and not judging their motivations. Work to empower them.

Resist the temptation to use fear of failure as a source of motivation. While it is not uncommon for a mentee to be motivated by fear, don't use fear to motivate. Rather, help walk your mentees through their fears. This is not to say that you shouldn't place the personal meaning of their goals against the consequences of not achieving them."

FEAR SHORT-CIRCUITS DEEP LEARNING

"For many procrastinating students, fear is their most powerful motivator, providing the adrenaline rush they secretly crave. They wait to study for an exam or write a paper until waiting any longer will ensure failure. Then they use fear to kick-start their academic motivation.

They use fear of failure, fear of humiliation, fear of disappointing family and friends, fear of diminished esteem in the eyes of others, fear of diminished self-esteem, fear of losing financial aid, fear of losing self-confidence, and fear of self-sabotage.

Students may successfully use fear to spur all-night studying for exams or writing papers, but fear used to overcome threatening educational obstacles does not foster reflective integration of what is learned with all that has been learned before. Fear truncates a student's education by limiting its reach and meaning.

Integration of learning occurs most readily when a student's mind is at peace with itself and the world at large. An un-roiled mind, one-pointed and interested, is able to integrate what is learned into long-term memory.

Fear does not attract interest in a subject, and it is interest that allows a student's mind to concentrate effectively on schoolwork. It is interest that creates a memorable education that expands exponentially throughout a student's lifetime."

MOTIVATING MOTIVATION

"College provides a unique opportunity for students to discover what motivates them most profoundly. Intrinsic motivation (for example, fulfilling one's potential and life purpose) is a deeper well to draw from than extrinsic motivators (i.e., a future career, pleasing parents, etc.). Intrinsic motivators are better able to change negative habits and behaviors into positive ones. As these habits and behaviors change, students can sense, pursue, and realize their potential more fully. Your job as mentor is to help make this happen.

Among your many goals is to help mentees discover and use their most personally meaningful life purpose to ignite intrinsic motivation that will lead to necessary action, even when the action is less than inspiring. As intrinsic and extrinsic motivators weigh in, value and life balance are found.

For an academically inactive mentee to become academically active and dedicated to schoolwork, the mentee must be willing to make sacrifices of time and social possibilities, deferring pleasurable or relaxing activities for the relative displeasure of struggling with academic work.

Help your mentees understand why the required sacrifice and self-discipline are worth it. Discuss their motivating purpose. How strong is their willingness to sacrifice for the successful life they want in the future, and the successful life they want now?

Motivation that results in timely and successful academic actions is motivation that gains momentum and strength with each success. Seize the day—*every* day—out of sheer gratitude, if nothing else. Of course there are as many reasons to seize the day as there are eyes that see.

What are your mentees' most compelling dreams for themselves? How do they want to *be* as they create their future? Embedded in the answers to these questions are powerful sources of motivation to achieve goals. Those who strive to live the spiritual qualities expressed by the Dalai Lama—'love and compassion, patience, tolerance, forgiveness, contentment, and a sense of harmony'—become inspirited, which is motivation in its purest form.

The present is key to the future. It is as important how we *be* as what we *do*. Once your mentees have uncovered their reasons for being, ask that they imagine their everyday life as an opportunity to live their reasons for existence.

Working consciously to be the person a student wants to be is as important as working to achieve a desired career. What qualities would your mentees have to embody to be someone they would admire?"

TIME MANAGEMENT

"What an interesting concept. Only humans with their ego-selves think they can manage time. It's odd. Though we think we're managing time, no one knows exactly what we're managing. After all, does anyone know what time is? I don't think so. All we know is 'what time it is.'

Thomas Mann wrote in *The Magic Mountain*, 'What is time? A mystery, a figment—and all-powerful. It conditions the exterior world, it is motion married to and mingled with the existence of bodies in space, and with the motion of these. Would there then be no time if there were no motion? No motion if no time? Is time a function of space? Or space of time? Or are they identical?' (437).

Now there's a take on time I'd like mentoring program supervisors, mentors, and mentees to consider!

The commonly held perception of time, found in *Webster's New World Dictionary*, is that time is 'the specific, usual, or allotted period during which something is done.' Or 'a precise instant, second, minute, hour, day, week, month or year, determined by clock or calendar.' But what exactly is being determined by clock or calendar? And does time become timeless through non-linear prayer, meditation, reverence, or dreaming?

Time is as mysterious and indefinable as gravity (a 'force' of 14.7 pounds per square inch).

What we do know about time, a human construct, is that there are 168 so-called 'hours' in a so-called 'week.' That's what we can manage our lives around. Whatever time is, it 'passes' whether or not we're managing it. All we can really do is manage ourselves in relation to time.

Our lives and the way we lead them are controlled by something we can't see, taste, touch, hear, or smell. We don't know what time is but we know we have a finite amount of it, which we often casually waste. Some mentees may even have a rebellious attitude toward time pressures which will manifest as procrastination.

Time is culture-specific. Some cultures experience time through the cyclical life-death-life-death of Hindu belief. Others experience it through the Buddhist Void or the time-filtering anticipation of the coming Rapture.

Many ancient cultures measured time cyclically through the successive, cosmically rhythmic day and night, rising and setting stars, waxing and waning moon, and changing seasons. A few twenty-first-century cultures still measure time this way.

Most contemporary cultures in our speed-of-light, information/technology age experience time linearly, cradle-to-grave, with competitive education and/or money-oriented time-perspectives. These cultures, which are dominant cultures on our planet, time-condition us from birth, placing us on well-timed feeding and sleep schedules. Before long, we're on play and learning schedules determined by our parents and early childhood educators.

When we're old enough to have playmates, we play timelessly until stopped by adults who return us to the world of their time. As children, our first impressions of time determined by others are often negative. When we don't behave well, we're given a 'time out.' In the evening, regardless of whether we're having fun, it's 'time for bed.'

Though teenagers assert time control to greater degrees in high school, their natural biological time, the time that in a wise and responsive society would be what determined when school began and ended each day, is largely ignored. The body-time of teenagers is attuned, if not biologically programmed, to stay up late and awaken mid-morning. This reality is ignored by high schools nationwide that routinely begin classes at eight. The school system certainly wasn't designed by someone under twenty-one.

To help your mentees not lose time because they are too overwhelmed by the enormity of a class assignment, break the challenging project into manageable everyday tasks that can be accomplished through to completion.

For many, if not most of your mentees, helping them schedule their time will be one of your most important jobs. Each person's relationship with time is highly personal and often only partially known. Help your mentees discover more about their relationships with time. Understand your own relationship with time."

TIME REBELLIOUS

"I remember during my early teen years, I was time-rebellious. If my parents wanted me to do something, I'd find a way to not do it or put it off until the very last minute. I wanted to do things when I wanted to do them. Everyone wore a watch but me. I disliked the idea of time ticking away on my wrist. The nature of time had changed from timeless baseball games played after school with neighborhood kids, to coming home from school and feeling I should be studying, even if I didn't want to. I longed for the time when I played baseball until the ball got lost in the twilight sky.

Once parents and numerous daily high school classes aren't monitoring their whereabouts, first-year students are emancipated from the time containers they've been in since birth.

Can students afford to be in a loose relationship with time? Perhaps some can, but most can't. The demands of academic life are simply too great for a cavalier attitude toward time.

At the end of the day and the end of the week, mentees can judge their relationship with time objectively through their achievements or lack of achievements. They can determine if opportunity has been lost. They can see the pattern and consequences of their time habits from week to week, and before long they will recognize habits that help and habits that harm.

Sometimes students proclaim their independence through uncensored behavior that acts as an emancipation proclamation to themselves and others. At last, no one to tell them where to be and when. They can go to classes or not go. Weeks can pass before some teachers even notice that a student hasn't been coming to class.

With an average course load of fifteen hours a week, the first-year student has most of her time free. It is not surprising that many are unable to balance studying, reading or writing time, and social time. It is understandably difficult for first-year students to say no to a party or a chance to get to know someone new when they should study but they have no friends."

> **Activity:** Have mentors close their eyes for an exercise. Tell them to raise a hand when they think five minutes have passed. Ask that they not count seconds during this exercise. Note the elapsed time when each opens eyes and raises a hand.

> **Discussion:** Ask how they experienced time without a timepiece to guide them.

A SELF-FULFILLING CONTAINER

"Before you meet with a mentee, know what you want to accomplish. During your meeting, while working toward your mentoring goals, discover what else you need to accomplish and enlarge your objectives accordingly. Mentor/mentee meetings need a structure, a container for achieving goals, but with breathing room.

The natural flow of your mentoring meetings should include certain basics that mentees can expect to discuss every time you meet. These basics are your mentoring 'center of gravity' and should be given attention every week, including their Seven-Day Plan's successes and setbacks; their Mind, Body, and Spirit Checklists, current short and long-term class requirements; time and self-management; memory, reading, note and test taking; and the impact of social life on academic life.

This snapshot of the last seven days and days to come is used to make necessary adjustments when co-creating the next Seven-Day Plan. What was the actual balance of time devoted to mind, body, and spirit?

Each mentoring meeting should have a structure, while allowing for unexpected situations requiring immediate attention. Allow time in meetings to include discussion of unsettling experiences and situations that have potential or current impact on a mentee's academic stride. Have the wisdom to be flexible enough to allow for the unscheduled, which will shape, to greater and lesser degrees, the success of each Seven-Day Plan.

What were the distractions? Talk about them. Revitalize motivation and focus. Have mentees make a personal agreement with themselves to achieve their goals for the next seven days. Doing so will strengthen their academic will.

41

At the beginning of your meetings with mentees, give some details about how you will spend time together. This is particularly helpful for students who need more structure and are not comfortable without a preview of the meeting they are about to have. Their degree of comfort usually increases after they learn to trust the mentoring process and get to know their mentor.

Mentors will meet with mentees once a week each week for an hour, unless you both decide two half hour sessions are preferable. Whether you meet once or twice a week is up to you and your mentees.

Three out of every four weeks, you will meet with me for a half hour and use another half hour to prepare for your mentees. Once a month we will meet as a group. I'll let you know where and when. Without ever naming our mentees, during these meetings we will discuss difficult mentoring situations and exchange group suggestions for how to best handle them.

It is important to have copies of all your mentees' syllabi. Make copies for yourself as soon as possible. Students often misplace their syllabi, so make sure they keep them in a notebook or notebooks. In the Fogolson Library you can make copies of any mentoring-related material. Ask for a copy machine card at the front desk. They'll have your name on a mentor list."

THE SEVEN-DAY PLAN

A goal without a plan is just a wish.—Antoine De Saint-Exupery

"The Seven-Day Plan is an agreement. The mentee who makes the plan with her mentor agrees to make every effort to follow the plan and achieve its goals. The weekly plan is a cornerstone of a student peer mentoring program, a schedule for actions to be taken. It is a great tool for success, but only if the mentee makes an agreement with herself to honor the importance of the plan by carrying it out.

In the final ten to fifteen minutes of your mentoring meetings, consider your mentees' academic, social, and spiritual needs for the next seven days and work them into their Seven-Day Plans. Their goals should be stated clearly and prioritized.

You are a team. Your dynamic should be an alliance, supportive and non-threatening. As a team, collaborate and create a Seven-Day Plan each week.

Speculate about potential obstacles. What might happen to derail your mentee's plan? Has a pattern of weekly derailments emerged? Develop a strategy to counteract what might prevent a mentee from succeeding during the next seven days.

Consider using the ABC Method: create three columns (A, B, and C) where 'A' is things that need to get done (i.e., where there's an obligation to get these things done), 'B' is things that should be done (things you feel are important but not necessarily front burner), and 'C' is things you want to get done but won't lose any sleep over if you don't—C is what you get to last.

Estimate the time each activity is going to take and check to see if you used more time, the time you thought you needed, or less time.

Offer your mentees copies of the following forms I created. For mentees who use one of these forms, I suggest they write in their fixed schedules, i.e., classes, job, housekeeping chores, and make copies that they use when co-creating their Seven-Day Plans."

Weekly Schedule Form

Name: _____   **Date:** _____

	MORNING	AFTERNOON	EVENING
Monday			
Tuesday			
Wednesday			
Thursday			
Friday			
Saturday			
Sunday			

Seven-Day Plan

Name: _____ **Date:** _____

Class Name	Absences	Tardies	Estimated Grade	Received Grade	Comments

Weekly Goals/Plan
-
-
-
-
-
-
-
-

General Comments
-
-
-
-
-

EXAMPLE: Seven-Day Plan
Name: _____ Date: _____

Class Name	Absences	Tardies	Estimated Grade	Received Grade	Comments
Printmaking	*0*	*4*	*B*	*0*	*Midterm critique after break; having a little trouble understanding material, will talk with teacher.*
Art History / Modern Art	*0*	*2*	*C*	*Quiz 61%*	*Worried about grade on paper.*
Sculpture	*0*	*3*	*B*	*0*	*Going well, not behind.*
Architecture	*0*	*1*	*B*	*Presentation = B Quiz = 0*	*Going well, but having trouble with reading.*

Weekly Goals/Plan
- Modern Art articles: read for Friday
- Study for Modern Art midterm Wednesday
- Go to Study Group w/ Justine Monday 6:00 p.m.
- Read for Architecture—prepare for quiz (take notes on reading)
- Talk to Justine about meeting after spring break
- Get a head start on research for Architecture presentation (due in April)
- Start sculpture presentation (slides/chap. in book) due April 5
- Architecture: research/write thesis for Louis Sullivan paper (due May 13)

General Comments
- *Primitive Art paper was hard, worked on it with 2 tutors, am worried about grade*
- *Project w/ Amy postponed until April*
- *Having trouble not procrastinating*
- *No Architecture midterm*
- *Going to stick with 13 credits each semester—don't want to get overwhelmed*

Student Daily Log Form

Name: _____ **Date:** _____

	Monday	Tuesday	Wednesday	Thursday	Friday	Saturday	Sunday
7:00am							
7:30							
8:00							
8:30							
9:00							
9:30							
10:00							
10:30							
11:00							
11:30							
12:00pm							
12:30							
1:00							
1:30							
2:00							
2:30							
3:00							
3:30							
4:00							
4:30							
5:00							
5:30							
6:00							
6:30							
7:00							
7:30							
8:00							
8:30							
9:00							
9:30							
10:00							
10:30							
11:00							
11:30							
12:00am							
12:30							

"Some mentees will prefer to use a hand-held device with a screen to schedule what they will do each day and when they will do it. Life today is largely lived in front of a screen. Other mentees will choose to create their Seven-Day Plans on a computer, preferably a laptop, which can be used during a mentoring meeting.

Students who are most comfortable in front of a computer may prefer to use a 'get things done' software application. When www.lifehacker.com asked viewers to submit their favorite get things done applications, of the five top favorites, 'pen and paper' came in first with 38.8 percent of the vote. Why do I find that so reassuring?

Some mentees will want every aspect of their next seven days planned; others will want a less controlling plan. Be sensitive to how comfortable your mentees are with their Seven-Day Plans. If they use one of the forms I offer, have them block out times (a different colored highlighter to outline when each class meets) and (same color as each class) block out corresponding study and work-on-assignments times.

Whichever form, daily planner, or electronic device your mentees choose, their Seven-Day Plans should take into consideration what was accomplished the previous week and their priorities for the week ahead. Their goals should be designed as blueprints for success, with achievements noted supportively and experienced as incentives for future success.

The following forms were created by Express Coaching of Vancouver, BC, Canada. The first, Formula for Achieving Goals, is especially useful for attaining short-term goals. The second, Five Planning Questions, works well for achieving longer-term goals, for example, when mentees are challenged by a major project or research paper. The third is a Contract with Self to establish a more personal commitment to the Seven-Day Plan."

Formula for Achieving Goals

A goal is created three times. First, as a mental picture of something you want to be, have, or do. Second, when written down to add clarity and dimension. And third, when you take action towards its achievement.

Mix one clearly-defined goal with three solid reasons why you want to achieve it. Then add specific actions you will take along with target dates for completion and you'll have a great plan of action.

GOAL—Write your goal in specific, measurable, and time-bound language.

_____

_____

WHYS—Identify and prioritize three reasons why you want to achieve your goal.

1. _____

2. _____

3. _____

ACTIONS—List specific actions and target dates to achieve your goal.

Action   Target Date
_____

Action   Target Date
_____

Action   Target Date
_____

Five Planning Questions

Use *What, Why, How, Who,* and *When* questions to help you clarify your goal, deadlines, and corresponding action items.

WHAT—is the specific goal that you want to achieve?

_____

WHY—do you want to achieve this goal?

_____

HOW—will you achieve this goal?
List each individual action step and deadline:

_____   _____
_____   _____
_____   _____
_____   _____
_____   _____

WHO—will be involved in helping you achieve this goal?
Identify each:

_____
_____
_____

WHEN—will you achieve this goal?
Identify a specific date:

_____

"Ask your mentees directly: *What do you need this week? What do you need to do?* Mentors, help your mentees meet their needs proactively. As Mick Jagger once advised, 'You can't always get what you want, but if you try sometime, you just might find, you get what you need.' He sure got that right.

The Seven-Day Plan should help your mentees create a healthful balance and integration of academic, social, and spiritual life. Their individualized plans, week after week, are a series of road maps to their destination—graduation.

Each meeting should conclude with mentees confident they can meet the challenges of the next seven days, armed with a written plan of action, a schedule, and the motivation to achieve it.

Of course, even the best Seven-Day Plans are ineffective if not used consistently, a dedicated practice week after week. The best of intentions may weaken without a strong commitment to follow through and successfully complete all aspects of each weekly plan.

Some students may need more than the Seven-Day Plan forms I've offered. Some may need a contract with the aspect of themselves to which their personal honor, their word is attached—a Contract with Self (or self). My mentor training embraces self-knowledge as a first step toward self-management.

Express Coaching offers the following Contract with Self to establish personal commitment. Unlike the other forms, this contract is about self-honor, whether the honor is in relationship to a higher power or to one's ego self."

Contract with Self

State your goal here:

_____

_____.

I,_____,hereby commit to achieving the goal that I have named above. I will plan thoroughly, act boldly, and be accountable for my actions.

I will focus on results and reinforce the values of discipline, character, and perseverance until success is achieved.

I will make sure that everything I think, say and do counts.

I will achieve this goal!

Sign your name here:

_____

Date:

_____

Activity: Have mentors fill out a Seven-Day Plan. Are they willing to sign a Contract with Self?

Discussion: Would you use one of these forms? What do you like or not like about them? What do you currently use to create your own Seven-Day Plan? Do you make an agreement with yourself to follow your plan and achieve its goals?

"For the Seven-Day Plan to be responsive to the priorities of your mentees, it is important to know how they are doing in their classes. This will give you much of the information needed to adapt Seven-Day Plans to current needs. Your mentees are on academic probation. Whether or not they are allowed to continue at the college next semester will depend on their grades this semester.

Do mentees have the right to not discuss their grades with you? They do, and they don't have to tell you how many absences or tardies they have, either. However, knowing their academic standing in each class is highly desirable. If they are reluctant to tell you their grades, ask if they would tell you if they receive any grades below 'C.' If they would rather not, respect their right to privacy and be responsive to their priorities. Regardless, professors of mentees who are failing a class will send an early alert to the dean who will forward it to me for follow up.

Most importantly, the Seven-Day Plan is created each week to set goals and a timetable for achieving them. It is an action plan for mind, body, and spirit. We want mentees to have a college life that is balanced between school work and social life, doing, and being (and becoming.)

A balanced student life addresses psychological, emotional, physical, and spiritual needs so untended needs don't distract from the primary quest at hand—being a successful student. A balanced, satisfying life makes it easier to concentrate for extended periods of time.

Shifting your mentees' priorities, intentions, and commitments to create disciplined actions may be necessary and that is what mentoring is at its best. The Seven-Day Plan is an action plan. Every item that is written on a 'to-do' list is an action item, even the most mundane chore. It takes action to complete it.

Studying is an action. So is going to class and making friends. An action-oriented person is not a person prone to procrastination, which feeds on inaction. The intention of every Seven-Day Plan is to achieve holistic success for mind, body, and spirit.

Some of your mentees may perceive themselves as passive students, doing as little as possible to get by. We want to help them think of themselves as always taking action in their best interest and the best interests of our college community. We want to help them actualize their potential through conscious, wise choices and alignment with their highest good and the highest good of those around them.

Everyone has the potential to achieve their highest good on any given day, but it requires conscious decision-making and sacrifice. A student has to decide to achieve her goals, even when she doesn't feel like it. She has to make sacrifices, the way all successful students make sacrifices.

If, on occasion, doing the 'next right thing' is having a cup of coffee with someone she's interested in, even if she has scheduled study time, go for it. She has her A, B, and C priority list in her Seven-Day Plan, so one way or the other she has to balance it and make up the time.

I would never argue in favor of ignoring 'kismet,' though it is important to acknowledge that every promising social situation isn't necessarily kismet. Many faux kismets turn out to simply be distractions.

You don't want your mentees to feel that nothing is going right because a few things go wrong. No one can predict unexpected intrusions. One of your many jobs as mentors is to talk non-judgmentally about the difference between welcome and unwelcome, avoidable and unavoidable distractions.

As the semester progresses, you should find your mentees increasingly inspired. You can measure your success by whether they are confidently stepping up to their challenges, using their one hundred and sixty-eight hours each week with greater awareness and care.

The Seven-Day Plan facilitates success. When mentees act every day to achieve their goals, week after week, less desirable habits turn into desirable ones. This doesn't necessarily mean they get all A's. It means they now have the habits of good students, committing time and effort.

In addition to the Seven-Day Plan, make sure your mentees have a large format desk calendar or a tabbed monthly calendar that fits into a three-ring planner. It is important that they refer regularly to a visual representation of how many days before an assignment is due or an exam given. If they're taking fifteen credit hours, what does thirty hours of reading, research, writing papers, and studying for quizzes and exams each week look like on a calendar?

When your mentoring meetings end, you and your mentees should have copies of their Seven-Day Plans and they should have high-energy motivation to achieve their goals. Keep copies of Seven-Day Plans in individual mentee folders so we can follow their progress from week to week. Extend your support by inviting them to phone or email you during the week if difficulties arise."

BELIEVE IN THEM

It's never too late to be what you might have been.—George Eliot

"If mentees don't achieve many of the goals of their Seven-Day Plans, don't be personally disappointed and don't despair. Explore the whys of the week that was, adjust their plans accordingly, and inspire them to do better during the next seven days. If you consistently believe in them, sooner or later they will start believing in themselves."

> **Activity:** Mentors, write five beliefs you have about yourself, and three different beliefs that others have about you.

> **Discussion:** Why should your mentees believe in you?

A WAY OF BEING

"Our goal is to create a mentoring program that will help empower mentees to be proactive rather than reactive toward their education and their lives. Express a proactive approach toward each mentee's learning and life, as well as your own.

In addition to being proactive, participate in the mentoring program you co-create—'everyone in the pool.' Mentors, create your own program of awareness and self-management paralleling the program you create with your mentees. Being proactive is particularly important in our culture where indifference and inertia are commonplace."

Proactive Mentor	Reactive Mentor
Co-creates effective, balanced Seven-Day Plans with mentees	Waits until a mentee problem arises, then responds
Develops caring, authentic, inspiring, trusting relationships	Mirrors the interest, commitment, and energy level of each mentee
Anticipates and addresses mentees' problems before they become crises	Allows mentees to set agenda and pace of mentor meetings
Models a positive attitude and disciplined, effective study habits	Is guided primarily by grades when determining mentees' needs
Acts as director of academic support for mentees with the goal of shifting responsibility for seeking academic, financial, social, and/or spiritual support from mentor to mentee	Ignores mentees' indirect signaling for help because it is not spoken directly

CO-ACTIVE, CO-PARTICIPATIVE

"Student peer mentoring program Seven-Day Plans are designed to be co-active and co-participative. By mentoring themselves while they mentor their mentees, mentors experience the same accountability they ask of their mentees. In doing so, they are living examples of the traits they wish to instill in their mentees."

Factors that Support Co-Participation	Factors that Interfere with Co-Participation
Equality and a shared mission	Inequality
Co-participation as a stated goal of all mentor/mentee meetings	A need to over control or over emphasize mentee weaknesses
Co-created Seven-Day Plans	Bad chemistry between mentor and mentee

"The coach is also a player. The art of peer mentoring is crafted from a shared purpose."

CHAPTER FOUR

Mentor Workshop Training

AN INSEPARABLE PROCESS:
FOUR INTERRELATED SKILLS

"Today's mentoring workshop and training is holistic, philosophical, and practical in approach. This segment is clearly practical, highlighting four subjects that are key to the success of everyone in our mentoring program: memory, reading, note taking and test taking. For your mentees to achieve their potential, they need to sharpen these important components of academic life.

During your mentoring meetings, teach your mentees techniques that will help them increase their abilities to recall at will, read effectively, take good notes, and do well on exams.

The academic needs of many students on academic probation often source back to one or more weaknesses in these four areas. It was with this in mind that just before Spring semester ended, I lent you copies of *Becoming a Master Student* by Dave Ellis, and asked that over the summer you read the chapters 'Memory,' 'Reading,' 'Notes,' and 'Tests.' I asked that you take your own notes on these readings and bring them to this workshop/training.

My estimate of your reading and note taking time is four hours, so remember to add this time to your mentoring hours when you fill out your first employment time sheet in two weeks. Weekly, you will be paid for each hour you meet with a mentee, as well as your half hour meeting with me, and a half hour prep time, when you will read pertinent material. Keep a record of what you read."

Discussion: Mentors will share their notes and thoughts on memory, reading, note taking, and test taking. They will discuss how they plan to mentor these subjects.

"Here are some of my own notes and excerpted sources regarding these four talents. I consider memory, reading, note and test taking as interrelated, foundational aspects of a single, inseparable process that, when mastered, leads to student success."

MEMORY

"Does anyone know for sure what memory is? We know its characteristics, how it behaves, and its dramatic range of capability. But do we know *what* it is? All we have are educated guesses, based on years of scientific and psychological tests telling us that sensory stimuli are received in our short-term memory but are stored there briefly. Within twenty-four hours, most people lose more than 85 percent of what they've stored in short-term memory. This has obvious implications for recalling information received during a classroom lecture or discussion, and for being able to remember what one reads, more than twenty-four hours later.

Unless deliberate steps are taken to guide a short-term memory from its temporary storage, through preparation for long-term memory, to long term-memory with infinite storage capacity, chances are a short-term memory will soon disappear.

I would like you to continue to read *Becoming a Master Student* throughout the semester, as well as *Essential Study Skills* by Linda Wong. Both are great resources. Be guided to relevant chapters in each by the results of your mentees' LASSI scores, their discussions with you, and feedback from returned class papers and exams.

I have copies of *Essential Study Skills* in my office and you can borrow it for short or long periods of time. In addition to the excellent chapter on memory in *Becoming a Master Student*, I suggest you read about memory in *Essential Study Skills*. Here are two excerpts:

The Information Processing Model
1. Our senses take in information, or sensory input
2. Our short-term memory receives the information and holds it briefly

3. We rehearse the information we want to learn
4. If we get feedback that we are not learning what we rehearse, that information goes through the feedback loop and returns to short-term memory for re-processing
5. Information that is adequately rehearsed moves into long-term memory, where it is permanently imprinted
6. Information stored in long-term memory is accessed through long-term retrieval—the output shows that we've learned (31)

Twelve Memory Principles
- **Selectivity** involves selecting what is important to learn
- **Association** involves associating or linking new information to something familiar
- **Visualization** involves picturing in your mind the information you are learning
- **Effort** on your part is essential for learning
- **Concentration** is necessary when you study
- **Recitation** involves repeating information verbally in your own words
- **Interest** must be created if it does not already exist
- **Big and little pictures** involves recognizing levels of information
- **Feedback** in the form of self-quizzing checks your progress
- **Organization** involves logical reordering of information
- **Time on task** refers to the time dedicated and scheduled for learning
- **Ongoing review** promotes practice retrieving information from memory" (42)

Successful students have learned how to consistently move attained knowledge from short-term memory to long-term memory. What facilitates this movement? A calm, centered, focused mind; a relaxed sense of confidence and well being; comprehensive preparation; finding personal meaning; and use of a preferred learning style when taking notes.

While there are many exercises for increased exam-related recall, some, e.g., mnemonic devices, rhymes and songs, and the loci system, are 'tricks' geared to help remember test material, but trick-remembered information usually slips from short-term memory soon after an exam is handed in.

Of course, everyone has times when they're glad to have a trick up their sleeve.

To help move information, an understanding, an insight, from short-term to long-term memory, I recommend repeated review of notes and test material, day after day, alone and in focused study groups. This creates repeated neural pathways to the same information, deepening with each review of material."

READING

"I suggest when you work with mentees to strengthen their reading skills, use the muscle reading section of the chapter 'Reading' in *Becoming a Master Student*. Here is a summary of muscle reading. Use it yourself and teach it to your mentees. Check to see that they're practicing it each week.

Muscle Reading—a leaner approach
- **Preview and question**. Flip through the pages, looking at anything that catches your eye—headings, subheadings, illustrations, photographs. Turn the title of each article into a question. For example, 'How Muscle Reading Works' can become 'How does Muscle Reading work?' List your questions on a separate sheet of paper, or write each question on a 3 by 5 inch card.
- **Read to answer your questions.** Read each article, then go back over the text and underline or highlight answers to the appropriate questions on your list.
- **Recite and review**. When you're done with the chapter, close the book. Recite by reading each question—and answering it—out loud. Review the chapter by looking up the answers to your questions. (It's easy—they're already highlighted.) Review again by quizzing yourself one more time with your list of questions (128).

Students are often encouraged to highlight key passages of their textbooks and write key words, concepts, questions, and answers in the margins. Some students prefer not to write in the margins. These students would benefit from keeping a separate Reading Journal. Others may want to highlight passages in their textbooks, write in the margins, *and* create additional neural pathways by keeping a Reading Journal, perhaps using the following form I created."

Reading Journal

Date: _____

Reading Assignment: _____

Definitions of Key Words

Key Word: _____ Definition: _____

_____

Key Word: _____ Definition: _____

_____

Key Word: _____ Definition: _____

_____

Important Concepts:

_____

_____

_____

_____

Questions:

_____

_____

_____

_____

Answers to Questions:

_____

_____

_____

_____

How the reading connects with what I learned in classroom lectures and discussions:

_____

_____

_____

_____

What I still need to understand:

_____

_____

_____

_____

What I'm going to do about it:

_____

_____

_____

_____

NOTE TAKING

"We are a note-writing, note-leaving nation. Nationally, prior to texting, the greatest number of notes each day were left on refrigerator doors and answering machines. As we stretch into the twenty-first century, texting, Facebook, and tweeting have emerged as the dominant daily forums for notes.

We're practiced at writing notes, but far less practiced at taking notes in a classroom. It's difficult to listen attentively, comprehend what a lecturer is saying, and take notes, simultaneously. Not everyone can multi-task like that. It is important that you, as mentors, regularly check on your mentees' class notes and reading notes. Ask questions to learn whether they and you can make sense of what they've written, and whether they're using an easy-to-follow narrative expressed in an abbreviated way. Some note takers simply leave out vowels from their written notes. Note taking styles should be individualized but comprehensible to an outsider. Check their classroom and reading notes and help them use their preferred learning style.

I like the Cornell Note Taking System, or an adaptation of it *(see illustration)*.

Questions and Central Ideas	Note Taking
Comments	

The Cornell system uses an 8½ by 11 inch sheet of paper and divides it with lines into three sections: for 'Questions and Central Ideas,' a left-side column, 2½ inches wide from the top-left of the page to 2 inches from the bottom, where an intersecting line stretches across the page. The area below this line is labeled 'Comments.' The largest area, to the right, 6 inches wide by 9 inches high, is labeled 'Note Taking.' This note taking system is made easier when a student uses a loose leaf notebook with room for 8½ by 11 inch sheets.

Note taking requires a system of abbreviations and symbols. Make sure your mentees use a consistent system that works well for them. If they don't have an effective system, help them create one that is easy to reconstruct and understand after a class.

Train your mentees to be *active* note takers, personally involved in taking notes and reacting to them as if in dialogue.

Mind mapping and concept mapping are two visual forms of note taking. Mapping helps students see the relationships between and among ideas and key words. It may take some time for mentees to develop a most-preferred and most-successful form of note taking. Be patient but persistent. Mentor the process. Encourage experimentation with various note taking techniques, then ask your mentees to use what works best.

The note taking process starts with mentees observing how they observe. Which of their senses are most engaged in a classroom? Their eyes? Their ears? Their sense of touch as they take notes? Is their mind distracting them from focused alignment with their senses?

Successful students direct their attention in class so their sight and hearing are centered on the educational experience and opportunity at hand. This requires paying attention throughout a lecture, participating actively in discussions, and taking meaningful notes that separate central ideas and concepts from examples and supporting evidence. Urge your mentees to review their notes immediately after a class ends, and before it meets again.

Mentees should arrive in any class prepared with a notebook, pen or pencil, or a laptop. Good note taking is facilitated when they sit within easy voice-range and clear sight-range of their instructor, paying attention to cues regarding what is an important idea or concept, and what could be asked on an exam. If it is written on the board, or in a handout, take special note. This information will probably be referenced on the next exam.

If a student has trouble taking notes because of a learning disability, suggest the possibility of getting a note taker for a class through the Academic Resource Center."

TEST TAKING

"Students can use the following suggestions when preparing for exams and quizzes:

Test Taking Suggestions
- Stay current with all assignments, and review class and reading notes every day
- Actively seek and find answers to questions you have regarding lectures or readings
- Find meaning in what you are learning and replace negative, self-defeating thoughts with positive thoughts of self-worth
- Speak with your instructor before a test to learn how you can best prepare for it
- Write a day-by-day study plan for an exam, with study strategies
- Form or join a study group with classmates who are serious students
- Break study sessions into time segments that are long enough to accomplish goals
- Create your own tests before your class test and, if possible, read your instructor's tests from prior years
- Use mind and/or concept mapping and flashcards
- Use stress-reducing techniques and maintain a balanced, harmonious life

The last tip is especially important. High test anxiety can undermine a student's ability to achieve success on tests, fracturing concentration, resulting in poor or failing academic performance. Many students under-perform on exams and quizzes because of self-defeating negative self-appraisals that result in disabling test anxiety. They catastrophize dire consequences if they do poorly or fail an exam. A realignment of perspective is needed. Life will continue much the way it has, regardless of the grade a student receives on an exam.

Mentors, if your mentees are test-anxious, in addition to teaching stress reduction techniques, e.g., working out at the physical fitness center, or breathing exercises, if appropriate, discuss whether they are making their self-esteem and self-worth part of what is being tested when they take an exam. Are they seized by irrational beliefs about their overall unworthiness? Do they hold themselves in low regard because they don't measure up to America's high-achievement ethic that makes losers out of those who aren't winners?

Remember, mentors and mentees: *you are not the grades you receive.* Your grades, cumulatively or singly, do not represent your value as a human being. You are infinitely greater than your grades, regardless of what they are. And yet, for many students, it is more than a stretch to believe that a poor or failing grade can be accepted as part of their education, small enough in the scheme of things to be minimized psychologically and emotionally.

Help your mentees develop perspective about their grades, regardless of what they are. Of course it is preferable to do well on an exam, but life is rarely turned upside down, *in reality*, because of a bad grade. Keep perspective and learn from each exam or quiz. Consider using the following form I created as a learning tool."

Analyzing a Returned Exam or Quiz

Course: _____

Date of Exam or Quiz: _____

Material Covered: _____

_____

_____

_____

Problem Areas (check if "Yes")

Testing skills:
- ☐ Misread or misunderstood the questions asked
- ☐ Didn't use time well
- ☐ Didn't directly and/or adequately answer the questions asked
- ☐ Unable to concentrate
- ☐ Mentally blocked

Test anxiety:
- ☐ Didn't use anxiety-reducing techniques
- ☐ Unable to access knowledge due to test anxiety

Comprehension and English skills:
- ☐ Didn't understand some vocabulary
- ☐ Reading speed too slow for time allowed
- ☐ Didn't understand lectures
- ☐ Inadequate knowledge of subject

Other: _____

_____

_____

_____

CHAPTER FIVE

Mentor Workshop Training

MENTORING HUMAN POTENTIAL

As we continue the workshop training from the previous chapter, we explore the nature and tools of mentoring and the program's holistic approach: mind, body, and spirit.

"Spirit responds best to passionate aliveness and is unresponsive to passive indifference, which is why bodies at rest tend to stay at rest.

Sometimes the amount of time students spend using their favorite high-tech immersions can surprise even them. Talk with your mentees about how much time they spend each day on Facebook, their cell phone, playing video games, texting, or surfing the Internet. Ask how much time they spend on their academic work. A heightened awareness is needed here. Is there an imbalance? If there is, ask what they think they can do to bring their imbalance into balance. Ask that they note how they spend their time each week.

Our goal is to transform mentees from less than successful students into successful, independent learners. The desired transformation requires that we start with 'what is,' the day-to-day reality of a student's academic, social, and spiritual life. 'What is' provides a base line for transformation. It establishes an honest, ongoing relationship with the academic strengths and weaknesses of each mentee. Change begins with self-acceptance and a desire to change.

We want to help mentees understand the direct relationship between their academic, social, and spiritual habits and their degree of academic success. We don't judge their habits but we do, when invited, explore whether their habits are having a negative effect on their schoolwork."

THE PACE OF CHANGE

"We've discussed 'time' and what mentees may have to give up to bring time management into balance—the forms and schedules required of the program, attention to meetings, and all the agreements about dedicating focus and time. When mentees get with the program, can positive change be far behind? Sometimes it can.

As mentors, it is natural to want positive change to occur quickly for your mentees, and on your watch. But please note: sometimes it's one step forward, two steps back. Sometimes mentees will accomplish the goals of their Seven-Day Plan for several weeks and then lapse for a few weeks and accomplish very little.

Negative academic and social habits are difficult to break, often re-emerging after positive habits have tentatively been established. This can be frustrating to a mentor who is doing everything 'right' and wants positive change to happen quickly.

Be patient. Sometimes one step forward and two steps back is progress. Sometimes, as Lao-tzu writes in the *Tao Te Ching*:

'The path into the light seems dark,
   the path forward seems to go back,
      the direct path seems long . . . .' (41)

You will draw on your own life lessons and rightly want to inspire your mentees, modeling and encouraging positive habits that will help them achieve the goals of their Seven-Day Plans while enjoying college life. After all, you changed, so can they. Maybe you procrastinated and now you don't. You want to share your story and you should do so, but don't be disappointed if you don't see an immediate payoff. Organic, lasting change has its own timetable, to be respected even when slow to happen.

For some, change is incremental and can be measured from week to week or month to month. For others, change occurs suddenly, after a long, slow buildup. As mentors, don't rush the pace of change for your mentees, though you are a catalyst for change every time you meet with them. Sometimes a mentee's low self-esteem will need a boost before he believes change is possible and his effort won't lead to failure and humiliation.

Of course the pace of change can be hastened when desire for change arises within your mentees with enough urgency so they will make the sacrifices necessary to turn self-limiting habits into self-realizing ones.

Change can be hastened through epiphanies that result in expanded awareness and gratitude for the educational opportunity at hand. And when change seems imperceptible, patience honors your mentees' autonomy, their freedom to change when *they* get it.

Sometimes there are aspects of our personalities that work against academic success and we may feel we are not ready to change them because these aspects may be an important part of who we think we are. Mentors' efforts may be at cross purposes with their mentees. If this is the case, and appropriate, talk supportively about your perception and ask if it is accurate. If commenting would be inappropriate, stay with your program. Appreciate each success and help make short-lived any indifference, slackening effort, or self-isolation from needed help.

And remember: the world is as you see it. Mentors who see the world through eyes that have successfully navigated the college's educational system have developed the confidence to override self-doubt and fear of failure. Mentees on academic probation haven't had this success and therefore see the demanding academic world around them as a place where they just might not measure up. Failure may loom as a real possibility, a self-fulfilling core belief."

THE LEARNING AND STUDY STRATEGIES INVENTORY

"To help you quickly understand how your mentees learn and study, you'll have them respond to the eighty statements in the Learning and Study Strategies Inventory (LASSI). Ask them to complete the LASSI during the week and bring it to your second meeting. You can score it with them then or later by yourself. During your mentoring meetings, work together to draw on their academic strengths and strengthen their weaknesses.

[I will give each mentor four Learning and Study Strategies Inventory profiles and a user manual written by Claire E. Weinstein, PhD, Department of Educational Psychology, University of Texas at Austin, and David R. Palmer, PhD, Texas Health and Human Services Commission.]

The LASSI takes about twenty-five or thirty minutes to complete and score. It reveals a college student's strengths and weaknesses in three essential areas: 'skills, will, and self-regulation.' Follow along in the user's manual while I read from my copy:

> 'The [LASSI] is a 10-scale, 80-item assessment of students' awareness about and use of learning and study strategies related to skill, will and self-regulation components of strategic learning. The focus is on both covert and overt thoughts, behaviors, attitudes, motivations and beliefs that relate to successful learning in post-secondary educational and training settings and that can be altered through educational interventions. Research has repeatedly demonstrated that these factors contribute significantly to success in college and that they can be learned or enhanced through educational interventions such as learning strategies and study skills courses.
>
> The LASSI is both diagnostic and prescriptive. It is designed to be used as
>
> - a screening measure to help students develop greater awareness of their learning and studying strengths and weaknesses
> - a diagnostic measure to help identify areas in which students could benefit most from educational interventions
> - a basis for planning individual prescriptions for both remediation and enrichment
> - a means for instructors to use for examining individual students' scores and class trends to help them decide where to place the greatest emphasis for assignments, projects, individual logs, journals, portfolios and other class activities
> - a pre-post achievement measure for students participating in programs or courses focusing on learning strategies and study skills
> - an evaluation tool to assess the degree of success of intervention courses or programs
> - an advising/counseling tool for college orientation programs, advisers, developmental education programs, learning assistance programs, and learning centers'

I like the LASSI. I think it gives a very useful profile of students' developed and underdeveloped learning and study strategies. When mentees sharpen their academic tools for success, their fear of failure lessens. With increased self-confidence they can more easily take on the daily challenges of academic life.

I'd like you to take and score a LASSI now so you have a profile of yourself as a student. You'll also have a sense of the accuracy of the LASSI in the ten subject areas it measures: attitude, motivation, time management, anxiety, concentration, information processing, selecting main ideas, study aids, self-testing, and test strategies."

Activity: Mentors will complete and score their own LASSI.

Discussion: Review LASSI results for accuracy or inaccuracy.

"Once you discover your mentees' academic and study strategies that need strengthening, read about the targeted areas in *Becoming a Master Student* or *Essential Study Skills*.

When we meet in my office we'll discuss your efforts to work with your mentees' LASSI profiles. To help your efforts I have information in my office about each of the ten areas assessed by the LASSI."

HOW WE LEARN

"Does anyone really know how we learn, how a cut heals, or what time is? Not really. But it is useful for you and your mentees to know how you learn best. In the not too distant past, theory held that our preferred learning style fell into one of three categories: auditory, visual, or tactile.

These general categories have merit, as well as limitations, since we are usually a balance of all three, with one learning style preferred. The merit is that once students know their preferred learning style, they can take steps to work with it.

Some students prefer an auditory style of learning, receiving, and processing information most effectively through hearing. These students can use audio tapes of lectures to supplement class notes. While this is very time consuming, for some it's just the ticket.

Soon after class, auditory learners (and all other learners as well) should review their notes by reading them out loud. And after reading an assignment (perhaps speaking as they read), they should summarize their reading, also out loud. It is important for auditory learners to sit in a classroom where they can clearly hear what their teacher is saying.

Visual learners prefer to use sight to receive and process material. These students should pay extra attention to any graphics in textbooks. They should draw pictures to illustrate their notes, use filmstrips and flashcards, and create mental pictures of concepts as a study/memory aid. Make reviews of test materials as visual as possible and suggest that they sit in classrooms where everything is in view.

Tactile/kinesthetic learners receive and process information most memorably through their sense of touch. These students learn best through activities that give them hands-on experience. When studying, they can benefit from tracing key words with a forefinger and writing out important facts and points of view several times.

Current theory holds that while these three general categories (auditory, visual, and tactile) are useful for students to explore, how we learn and learn best involves multiple intelligences and learning styles.

In 1983, in his book *Frames of Mind*, Howard Gardner theorized that humans have a range of at least seven different expressions of intelligence: verbal-linguistic, musical-rhythmic, logical-mathematical, visual-spacial, bodily-kinesthetic, intrapersonal, and interpersonal (73-256). Twelve years later, Daniel Goleman added "emotional intelligence" to the seven types of intelligence and learning.

This week, go online and take the Rogers Indicator of Multiple Intelligences. Consider the implications for yourself as a student. How can you use what you have learned? Have your mentees go online and do the same thing. Discuss the results.

Another style of learning is where in a classroom a student learns best. Though it is a commonly held belief that students learn best if they sit up front, preferably three or four seats to the left or right of center, for many students the place where they feel comfortable and can learn best in a classroom is as personal as choosing a seat in an uncrowded movie theater."

LEARNING PORTFOLIOS TO ENHANCE
AND RETAIN WHAT IS LEARNED

"My guess is if college graduates were given their senior year final exams a year after graduating, many, if not most, would fail them. Why? Because many, if not most classes are taught as separate units of knowledge, semester-long accretions of facts, points of view, and course-specific insights. Course material is not usually interrelated with other course material, prior knowledge, and understanding.

Students are infrequently asked to reflect on and integrate what they are being taught with their infinitely larger web of learned and experienced education, acquired through everyday interactions with humans and other living life forms.

What do mentees think about what they are learning? What do they feel about it? What does it mean to them? How does what they learn contribute to and enlarge their sense of self and life lessons distilled from the world they share?

Mentors, as you strengthen your mentees' academic skills and learning strategies, help them discover and understand the interconnectedness of all aspects of their education. Help them explore the personal meaning (or lack of meaning) of what they are learning. Through discussion, facilitate the integration of their newly acquired knowledge with what they have previously learned. By doing so, you will deepen the depth and evolving meaning of their education. These important goals are well served when your mentees develop learning portfolios.

John Zubizarreta writes in his book, *The Learning Portfolio*,

'The model I have proposed for the learning portfolio stresses the interplay among the three vital elements of reflection, evidence, and collaboration or mentoring. Sustaining the process of developing and revising the portfolio is the power of writing as a corollary to thinking and learning as well as a creative and facilitative activity for recording, assessing, improving, and evaluating learning. The learning portfolio, therefore, consists of a written narrative section in which the student reflects critically about essential questions of what, when, how, and why learning has occurred. In the course of such introspective analysis, the student is guided to think further about how specific acts of learning—for instance, a workshop or lab course, a special writing assignment in a class, a long-term undergraduate research project, a field experience or internship, an interdisciplinary core, or an honors program of study—have contributed to a coherent, developmental, interrelated process of learning (24).'

Learning portfolios should be creative, personal, and meaningful, a reflective contemplation of the process of learning. If your mentees want to create a learning portfolio (sometimes called a learning journal), help them develop and maintain one. Portfolios can use traditional media or can be created and maintained electronically on the Web.

Regardless of the method used, mentor the process. Tailor the scope and style to your mentees' available time, interest, and personal preference. Willing mentees will benefit from keeping a learning portfolio for each of their classes. If you, as mentors, keep learning portfolios yourself (I recommend you do), share some readings with your mentees from time-to-time.

On average, creating a learning portfolio takes about two hours per semester, if it is a mentor-initiated activity. Additional time may be necessary when portfolios are used in classes as independent projects or extra credit."

HABITS OF MIND

"The important questions of *what*, *when*, *how*, and *why* learning has occurred are directly or indirectly related to habits of mind. Many, if not most students don't ask these contemplative questions as they learn. Their approach to education is often passive, leaving it up to their teachers to give them the information needed to pass their exams. This approach is a habit of mind systematically shaped over many years of reactive learning, their curiosity held in check by testing and writing requirements.

Because of the limited personal meaning of a reactive, 'Is this going to be on the final?' approach to their education, your mentees may enter college feeling a disconnect between the classes they are taking and their 'real lives.' This disconnect may mute their intentions and efforts to interact with their college's faculty and staff in a deep and meaningful way, resulting in an un-integrated, soon-forgotten education.

An impersonally experienced education may result in self-defeating, negative habits of mind and these habits can become self-fulfilling prophecies. It is not uncommon for a struggling student to tell himself, 'You're too stupid to succeed. You've always screwed up. What makes you think things will be different now that you're in college?' Repeated negative self-talk may result in the student concluding, 'What's the use of knocking myself out? It's not going to make any difference.'

A student who is minimally involved educationally may set his academic bar low enough so that failure is an option. This attitude can justify a mentee not committing the necessary time, energy, and intention to do well in every class, even the boring ones. Learning portfolios foster involvement.

Mentors and mentees, ask yourselves: Which habits of mind produce actions or inactions that keep you from achieving your goals? Self-knowledge is necessary for transformation to occur."

You live in the fruits of your action and your action is the harvest of your thought.—Henry Miller

"What does your mind loop back to frequently during your days and nights? Do you spend time mind-obsessing about academic or social life situations without doing anything about them? What interrupts your ability to concentrate? For a student, the ability to concentrate on academics during time set aside for it is of paramount importance.

In his book, *How to Meditate*, John Novak quotes J. Donald Walters:

'Concentration is the key to success in every undertaking. Without concentration, thoughts, energy, inspiration, purpose—all one's inner forces—become scattered. Concentration is the calm focus of one's full attention on the purpose at hand. Concentration means more than mental effort: It means channeling your heart's feelings, your faith, and your deep aspirations into whatever you are doing. In that way, even the little things in life can become rich with meaning. Concentration should not involve mental strain. When you really want something, it is difficult not to think about it! Concentrate with interest on whatever you do, and you will find yourself absorbed in it (45).'

Mentors and mentees, reflect on habits of mind that have affected your success as students. *Which habits have you changed? Which habits would you like to change? What attracts the attention of your mind and why?*

Over many years of schooling, we've all learned and practiced habits that helped and habits that harmed. Take an inventory. *How do your positive habits of mind and action or inaction help you? How do your negative habits harm you? What are you willing to do about them?*

Procrastination, for example, is a habit of mind. We've all procrastinated at one time or another. Some of us were successful procrastinators, others were not. The successful procrastinator usually says, 'I don't do my work until the last minute because I work best under pressure.' This is true for some but not for most.

Procrastination can throw a student's life out of balance, to the point where the student fails or greatly underachieves. For every student who excels by waiting until the last possible moment to work on papers and projects, my guess is there are more than five who do average or below average work."

> **Activity:** On your pad, write a paragraph that completes this sentence: 'My success depends on . . . .' After ten minutes, have mentors read aloud their responses. This is a useful exercise for mentees as well.

REWRITE YOUR SUBCONSCIOUS LIFE SCRIPT

"Close your eyes for a minute. Witness and watch the thoughts and emotions that arise. They spring from a lifetime of subconscious cultural and life scripts that shape our expectations for ourselves. Mentors and mentees each bring to their college experiences the conditionings of their lifetime, including conditionings of mind.

We're patriots of this country because we've been conditioned to be patriots. Chances are most of us would be patriots in our most hated country if we were born there. We are the embodiments of our heritage, family, traditions, rituals, social manners and controls, expectations, intelligence, spiritual and economic perspectives and beliefs, to name some of the most influential.

Our cultural imprints shape what we do, what we believe and the way we live, revealing character through actions, speech, and thoughts, especially thoughts that cause students' minds to drift while feigning attention in class. The rapid-fire discursive thoughts of eighteen-year-olds are bred in a culture with an ever-shrinking attention span.

This is important to remember because in class, or when studying, if there is enough emotional charge to a student's thought, his mind will fix on it and expand its importance. The charged thought will share his mind's attention, resulting in intermittent listening in class."

DISTRACTIONS OF MIND

"Guide your mentees to recognize and non-judgmentally note distractions of mind that compete for attention while they listen in class, write a paper, or prepare for a test. Typically, the human mind chatters unheard except as an inner voice that sometimes commands the attention of a shout. Thoughts weave their way through our days and nights like a background movie that sometimes becomes a feature, occasionally even appearing as dreams during sleep.

Each week offers a parade of possible distractions that can turn out to be two steps backwards for mentees. What distractions did they allow? A friend? An enemy? A boyfriend, girlfriend, a parent? Money pressures? A misunderstanding in their dorm?

You can assume there were many daily distractions since you last saw your mentees. Were they able to stay focused on their schoolwork without multi-tasking stray daydream thoughts that arose? Did any distractions keep them from succeeding during the week? These are important questions that lead to self-knowledge, the wellspring for change.

Thoughts that distract from class time or study time are best given short shrift. Unrelated social thoughts allowed free reign are likely to interfere with the discipline, goal-oriented concentration and self-management necessary for a student to succeed.

Awareness of and dis-empowerment of distracting thoughts is part of self-management, necessary if a student wants to accomplish something meaningful during an hour's study time. We need to quiet our minds, be attentive, and cultivate our ability to concentrate for significant periods of time. A still but active mind can more easily sustain attention and keep motivation high, especially when aligned with Great Inventor Energy.

What can we do to control the thought preoccupations of our minds? First, observe the power and control our minds have over how our waking time is spent. Witness the emotions our thoughts evoke in us.

If your mentees are up for it, have them jot down brief notes of their mind wanderings during the week. I know most mentees won't want to do this but talking about it as a possibility will impart an awareness of its importance.

Suggest to your mentees that if they don't want to journal about high maintenance thoughts, they should bear witness as their thoughts pass through their interior mindscape. Ask that they watch their thoughts without judging or trying to stop them. This will teach how to weaken tangential thoughts and improve powers of concentration."

COGNITIVE DIRECTION

"The consequences of a student's distracted mind are often made most apparent when he has to work through the night because in previous weeks he was simply too distracted to do his work. It's easy for low self-esteem to set in after an unsuccessful all night effort. Negative self-perceptions create negative feelings and negative feelings can easily affect academic performance and social interactions.

If your mentees want to see their pattern of distractions during any given week, have them use the following distractions form."

Distractions Form

Name: _____ **Date:** _____

Class: _____

	STUDY/ WORK TIME	EFFECTIVE STUDY/WORK TIME	DISTRACTIONS
Monday			
Tuesday			
Wednesday			
Thursday			
Friday			
Saturday			
Sunday			

"What causes negative thoughts? Start with core beliefs, which can generate thought-habituated self-perceptions such as: 'I'm a loser,' 'No matter how hard I try I'm a failure,' 'No one likes me,' 'Nothing ever works out for me.' The feelings created by these core beliefs may include anger, frustration, confusion, and motivational paralysis. These feelings are counterproductive to successful academic and social life.

On infrequent occasion, a mentee's negative thoughts become all-consuming and their mental/emotional condition deteriorates to a state of holistic dysfunction, where mind, body, and spirit disengage from school work altogether. Your mentee is in crisis. You will want to help, and of course you should, but you shouldn't be *the* help.

Don't make your mentee's mental health crisis your responsibility alone. Talk to me about the situation and I'll meet with the troubled student and find the right primary help.

As mentors, your job is to give mentees the support and guidance they need to succeed, but it is necessary to know the boundaries of your work. If you have any questions about boundaries, ask me, your program supervisor. Mentoring requires close attention to what mentees need and sometimes those needs are beyond the appropriate reach of a mentoring relationship. Student peer mentors are not licensed therapists or counselors. Know and respect the boundaries of your job as mentor. What you can do is offer appropriate mentoring help, guided by our discussions."

BE LIFE AFFIRMING

"Over weeks and months, you can help yourself and your mentees create positive core beliefs by using personally meaningful, empowering affirmations. Affirmations are an effective way to harness the positive power of spirit and change negative core beliefs.

What is an affirmation? Dave Ellis writes in *Becoming a Master Student*:

'An affirmation is a statement describing what you want. The most effective affirmations are personal, positive, and written in the present tense. Affirmations have an almost magical power. They are used successfully by athletes and actors, executives and ballerinas, and thousands of people who have succeeded in their lives. Affirmations can change attitudes and behaviors. Affirmations commonly begin with the phrase *I, _____, am . . .*—for example, *I am courageous and successful.* Some affirmation aficionados believe the positive impact of affirmations increases when their origin drops from the mind to the heart. For example, *I, _____, am courageous and successful,* might become *I, _____, feel courageous and successful* (50).'

My perspective is that heart-centered affirmations can align a student with a higher power (or not). An example of a higher power alignment might be: *I, _____, feel the guidance of _____ (one's higher power) working for my highest good.* Or, *I, _____, feel spiritually motivated by the divine intentions of my soul.*

Examples of affirmations that do not invoke a higher power might be: *I, _____, feel motivated and dedicated every day to achieve my goals,* or *I, _____, feel worthy and capable of success.*

Affirmations help establish intentions and the will to achieve them. They are especially useful when spoken at the beginning and end of each day."

Activity: Mentors will write three affirmations. Follow with discussion of their affirmations.

"Mentors, ask your mentees to write three affirmations and discuss them together."

MIND-CREATED ATTITUDES AND BEHAVIOR

"Encourage your mentees to be grateful for the opportunity to receive and achieve a good education. Are they grateful? What are their attitudes toward their education? Are they eager to learn, or are they indifferent, turned off by bad high school experiences? These are important questions and only honest answers will allow you to create a program tailored to meet their needs.

Did your mentees slide by in high school because little was expected of them academically? Were they disciplined in their approach to schoolwork? Did they get the support they needed? What is their attitude toward tutoring or being mentored?

The psychological needs of college students admitted on academic probation can be acute and can affect their attitudes. No one is sure to succeed, so they often arrive in a state of anxiety, without friends to help them through. They may project an 'everything is under control' attitude when they don't think anything is under control.

Let your mentees know the Academic Resource Center should be an important part of their academic life. Introduce them to everyone at the center and urge them to use the support services frequently. Make sure they have a list of tutors and their phone numbers. When the help your mentee receives pays off in good grades, you're likely to see an improved attitude toward the educational experience offered by the college."

AND IF HIS SHOULDERS SHRUG?

"What should you do if you discover that one of your mentees is indifferent to his education? Work to change his attitude, of course, but how? The answer differs with each mentee. Examine the history and origin of his negativity. Have him talk about the cause(s) as specifically as possible and make 'caring about my education' one of the goals of his Seven-Day Plan.

It is surprising how many students I counsel have had negative high school experiences and arrive at the college with weighty psychological baggage. They don't want to be humiliated again and are often unfamiliar with what it feels like to be a student with a positive attitude toward education.

Some mentees may have an 'it's no big deal' attitude toward their college education because it wasn't cool in high school to study too much. Studious students may have been shunned as nerds. Others may have negative attitudes toward our educational system in general, thinking it too highly competitive, irrelevant, or boring.

A cynic might say the common objective of most students is good grades, not good education. I'm not a cynic and I would agree, noting sadly that grades are external motivators and after they are received, the subject matter for which they were given often fades as quickly as water on a desert.

A positive attitude toward education is highly desirable. Mentors, examine your own attitudes toward education and explore the subject with your mentees. Discuss past educational experiences and the effect of these experiences on their education today. Have hurtful memories lessened their self-esteem? Mentees may worry they will have similar experiences with their college professors and classmates.

Model a positive and honest attitude toward education. Encourage your mentees having academic difficulty to talk with their teachers. A positive attitude is one that respects the learning opportunity at hand and the hard-earned money paying for every class, even the boring ones.

In addition to discerning the attitude of a mentee toward his education, it is also important to be aware of your own attitude toward being a mentor, and your mentees' attitudes toward being mentored. A grateful attitude can intensify motivation and strengthen educational commitment."

MINDFULNESS

"Reducing the number of attention-diverting thoughts is an important goal that is key to using scheduled time well. We don't want to throw time away because our egos need mind-attention to work out insecurities that appear as unsettling thoughts.

Encourage mentees to practice mindfulness. Ask them, when studying or in class, to do a mind check every five to ten minutes to determine whether they're focused on academics. If their attention has wandered, suggest they say 'now' to themselves, a trigger to automatically return them to their school work. I like the word 'now' as a return-to-academics word because it brings the student back to the present where he is less vulnerable to intrusive thoughts. Now, the present moment, is where a mentee's mind can work most easily on the goals of his Seven-Day Plan.

John Milton wrote in *Paradise*: 'The Mind is its own place, and in itself can make a heaven of hell, a hell of heaven.' This is an important understanding for mentors and mentees. What kind of heaven or hell did we make for ourselves during the last seven days? Here is a weekly Mind Checklist that can be used to find out."

MIND CHECKLIST

Rate your last seven days from 1 to 5, with 5 as the highest rating:

_____ Your ability to focus on schoolwork at will for long periods of time

_____ Your self-image reflected through self-esteem and self-confidence

Your distractions from academics caused by
_____ competing, unrelated thoughts
_____ negative emotions
_____ dominating desires
_____ stress

Activity: Rate yourselves on the Mind Checklist.

Discussion: How do you use your mind? How does your mind use you?

HABITS OF BODY

"Is the human body an extension of the human mind? There is a respected school of thought that believes it is. What but the consciousness of mind keeps our hearts beating, our lungs breathing? Most people take involuntary body functions for granted but are these life essentials anything less than miraculous?

The human body is a quantum leap beyond anything humans can create: (e.g., 60,000 miles of blood vessels, a heart that beats 100,000 times every day, over a billion nerve cells, human eyes that can differentiate 10 million different colors, opposable thumbs, etc.).

Surely each body deserves great respect and attention to its needs. And yet it is not uncommon for college students to rivet their attention to their body's outer appearance while ignoring the needs of their inner body. Many party late, sleep little, eat on the run, and exercise infrequently, indifferent to what they put in their bodies.

Without sounding like a parent, increase your mentees' awareness of how they can take better care of their bodies. Build into each Seven-Day Plan a daily regimen that will strengthen their immune systems.

Lack of sleep and missed meals can weaken a student's immune system and heighten susceptibility to illness. For students who are socializing night owls, routinely up until the wee hours, lunch is often the first meal since dinner, eighteen hours earlier. It is difficult to concentrate in class when bleary-eyed and hungry. Coffee, colas, and vending machine snacks often become before-class quick fixes, attempts to compensate for lack of sleep and nutrition.

Results vary. Some sleep-deprived students run on forty winks and junk food the entire semester and do well. Most, however, slip by degrees and function with low energy that contributes to their procrastination. Some miss classes and on occasion fall too far behind to catch up.

Ask your mentees if their sleeping and eating patterns are affecting their ability to do well at the college.

Key to a well maintained student's body is exercise, even when stress is manageable. When it's unmanageable, as it is for many students before midterms and finals, the need for exercise, good food, and enough sleep becomes even more important. Make sure these essentials are tended to daily as part of your mentees' Seven-Day Plans."

REGARDING SEX, DRUGS, AND TEMPLES

"Decisions and behavior regarding sex and drugs have noteworthy impact on a student's body. But unless a mentee initiates conversation about either of these subjects, don't pry. Here are my keep-it-simple basics.

Regarding drugs and alcohol, a majority of college students indulge to a degree. The question is, to what degree? If a mentee shares that he is using illegal substances, and use is getting in the way of his schoolwork, what should you do? There is no pat answer. Some mentors will discuss the issue and offer guidance. Others will suggest their mentee make an appointment with the college drug and alcohol counselor.

It is good to know if drugs and/or alcohol are clouding a mentee's ability to think clearly and stay well, but respect your mentee's privacy. This information should come naturally from mentor/mentee conversation or it shouldn't come at all.

Whether and how often to use drugs and/or alcohol is a choice every college student faces. If you do discuss sensitive social issues, don't make these issues the unbalanced focus of your mentoring meetings. If lengthy discussion is needed by a mentee, suggest he set up an appointment with a mental health counselor.

Regarding sex, of course everyone should protect against unexpected pregnancies and STDs. And, if our bodies are temples, treat them accordingly. Make conscious decisions. As for mentor/mentee conversations about specifics, and/or a crisis, again, our college counselors have the training and credentials to handle highly sensitive issues professionally.

Of course, if drug/alcohol use is putting a mentee's life at risk, or if a mentee is putting another person's life at risk, let me know immediately. Short of that, your concern should be limited to the impact drugs and/or alcohol use is having on your mentee's ability to stay well and achieve academically."

BODY CHECKLIST

Rate your last seven days from 1 to 5, with 5 as the highest rating:

_____ Exercise/fitness

_____ Nutrition

_____ Hygiene

_____ General health

_____ Sleep

Activity: Rate yourselves on the Body Checklist.

Discussion: How do you tend to the needs of your body? Ideally, how would you tend to the needs of your body?

HABITS TOWARD SPIRIT

"Spirit is usually given short shrift as a priority in the curriculum and culture of college life. Consequently, my notes on the subject are more extensive than those on mind and body. Spirit is rarely explored in academia.

Mentoring should be a celebration of spirit, regardless of how spirit is perceived. Spirit has the ability to help the inspirited achieve what they dream and create as goals.

Let's assume, for the sake of discussion, that spirit exists as an all-pervasive—a power infinitely greater than any power humans think they have. Are we spiritual beings having a human experience or humans having a spiritual experience?

In the rare instance that a mentee experiences life as a spiritual being having a human experience, the mentor/mentee relationship may best be centered around the mentee's profoundly important spirituality. What would the meaning of a college education be to a spiritual being having a human experience? You would certainly want to find out.

Far more common are people who consider themselves humans having an occasional spiritual experience, often on Sunday morning. A recent survey of College of Santa Fe students found that seventy-five percent attended religious services with some regularity in their hometown. Many of these students derived strength and inspiration from their religious/spiritual practices but they often discontinue their practices when they begin their college education.

Talk to your mentees about whether they had a religious/spiritual practice at home and whether they want to find a similar practice in Santa Fe. A student in relationship with a higher power may gain strength, comfort, and serenity, all beneficial for achieving academic success. But be sensitive. Spirituality is a very private aspect of anyone's life. If a mentee isn't interested in discussing the subject, quietly back off; simply embody spiritual qualities and be expressions of them. If a mentee is interested in spirituality, ask if you can be of any help.

A higher power in any form, name, or religion can be an extraordinary motivator and stabilizing influence. Self-motivation may be most powerfully activated when self is infused with a higher purpose than the material world offers.

I hear you. What about students who don't believe in a higher power or the oneness of all? These students can be in relationship with their spirit if they perceive it as a secular, self-interest energy, actualized when they achieve personal goals. Honor any and all relationships your mentees have with spirit."

HEART OF THE MATTER

"In his book, *The Tao of Physics*, Fritjof Capra writes,

> 'In contrast to the mystic, the physicist begins his enquiry into the essential nature of things by studying the material world. Penetrating into ever deeper realms of matter he has become aware of the essential unity of all things and events. More than that, he has also learnt that he himself and his consciousness are an integral part of this unity. Thus the mystic and the physicist arrive at the same conclusion; one starting from the inner realm, the other from the outer world. The harmony between their views confirms the ancient Indian wisdom that Brahman, the ultimate reality without is identical to Atman, the reality within (296).'"

DUALITY AND MENTORING

"Almost all of us (including mentors and mentees), live our lives with dualism as our everyday experience of reality, as if we were separate from the rest of the universe. We experience ourselves as infinitely insignificant in the cosmic scheme of things, small in our daily lives, alone in the world. Dualism conditions practitioners to believe that their individual existence is separate from all other existences. They experience life accordingly, bound myopically to their psychological selves, which divide things into good and bad, greater and lesser, black and white. Though unacknowledged by most people, dualism distances us from the intimacy of our oneness with all life on earth.

Mentors who interact with their mentees non-dualistically, as expressions of spirit, will inspire and motivate them to similar ways of being and doing in the world. We are One, alive in a spirit-infused cosmos of infinite subatomic waves that can turn into particles, and particles that can turn into waves.

Consider this possibility: the divine manifests in everyone and everything as everyone and everything, responsive to human intention that actualizes the highest good—spirit. This understanding establishes a relationship with the universe that is highly personal and interactive. For mentors and mentees, their relationship or lack of relationship with the universe is worth discussing. Do they think the universe supports their intention to achieve envisioned, worthy goals? Or do they exist in an indifferent universe?"

THE DARK UNDERTOW OF INEQUALITY

"For mentors and mentees, a consequence of dualism's psychological distancing may be that they unwittingly fall into hierarchical mentoring roles, (mentor as Big Daddy or Mommy, mentee as Junior). These roles may create guarded mentor/mentee sharings of dimensional, authentic life, and may produce projected personae that seem appropriate for the separateness caused by dualism's fear-based perspective. Hierarchies foster inequality. Spirit is an expression of equality, perhaps because equality best expresses the reality of equal divinity in all, for all to enjoy.

Living without the illusion of separateness allows us to honor and resonate with the reality that we are all marginally different frequencies of the same infinite consciousness. Think of mentors as vibrantly struck tuning forks approaching less resolutely struck tuning forks—their mentees. We are all interconnected, swimming in an endless holy river of energy called spirit.

'I am he as you are he as you are me and we are all together,' John Lennon sang in 'I Am the Walrus.' Mentors and mentees are only seemingly separate when they meet. True, they assume mentoring roles and responsibilities, but on the deeper level of mystery, spirit, and love, all life is inseparable. Non-dualism is seamless, infinite reality. We are indivisible. You can *feel* alone but you can never *be* alone."

FROM THERE TO HERE WITHOUT MOVING

"Of course, mentors with dualistic world views can be as effective as those with non-dualistic perspectives. But consider: though there are dozens of important factors that contribute to effective mentoring, perhaps none can establish bonding between mentor and mentee more quickly and naturally than the experience of oneness through non-dualism.

In a cosmic nutshell, people who live life dualistically are prone to believe, 'I am separate from everyone and everything out there.' This false belief can lead to fear and suspicion, and often results in psychological and emotional distance between and among people, including mentors and mentees.

Non-dualism, on the other hand, makes six degrees of separation an illusion. There is no 'other,' which is the reality quantum physics has revealed to be true. We live in and as infinite energy that is the source of all creation. This is the same source that has been revered and illuminated by eastern sages and mystics for more than two thousand years."

WHAT WOULD HAPPEN?

"What would happen if educators, media, teachers, and parents were to publicly recognize and teach non-dualism as a universal truth? Peace just might break out. And love. And school connectedness. People might find themselves looking into their own eyes through the eyes of everyone they meet. The intimacy and universality of this experience might cause them to pay homage each day to their honored place in the eternal cosmic body of consciousness.

With regard to mentoring, if non-dualism was taught in schools at all levels, mentors and mentees would establish mutuality and trust more easily because the relationship would be one in which respect and relatedness would flow in both directions, without the implicit hierarchy that dualism spawns.

Intra-personal hierarchies are foundational in our society's educational pedagogies. Dualism is a widely accepted Western perspective and a philosophical model for educating students. The result? Competition dominates cooperation, and for most students, the teacher, separated psychologically from students, is seen as authority, minister of rewards and punishment, exemplar of objectivism. It is memorable when a teacher imparts knowledge, wisdom, insights and uplifting ways of being. Students are infrequently taught how to help create and participate in a supportive, loving, educational community.

Emphasizing knowledge and know-how, most educators present a world view that repeatedly separates the inseparable: the observer and the observed. For students, conforming to the passive protocol of most classrooms, the world becomes what they are taught, and the meaning of much of their education is centered on words like 'theory,' 'facts,' and 'logical analysis.'

In a non-dualistically-oriented classroom, students are more inclined to share a collective recognition that they are in a learning community made stronger and more educational by diverse opinions and a communal approach to learning. This approach teaches the relatedness of subject matter to other subject matter, and students to other students.

When teachers celebrate their shared gift of life with students, regardless of what they are teaching, classroom separation (student and teacher) is diminished and it becomes easier for a student to meet with his instructor. What they share in common is considerably more significant than their teacher/student roles and differences. It's a matter of perspective.

A non-dualistic approach to education uses theories, facts, and logical analysis, but doesn't turn them into dominating conclusions. They are valuable contributors to a dimensional and meaningful education that embraces an everyday awareness of the invisible complements to the visible world. This is where spirit dwells most exuberantly, and can enliven most directly.

Does this really matter when mentoring? It does. Our perception of reality and our aloneness or connectedness can greatly influence our ability to achieve a deep and ever-expanding education. Spirit motivates and inspires, all but unrecognized as a powerful academic support.

Regarding mentors and mentees and the inherent equality of non-dualism, some may assert there has to be respect for authority and this respect and necessary accountability can only be accomplished through clearly defined, hierarchical roles of mentor and mentee, even if perceived dualistically. I disagree. Hierarchies breed fear, which can inhibit and/or undermine a mentor/mentee relationship. Non-dualism fosters equality consciousness, an ideal environment for building trust when mentoring.

With trust, our shared human condition, lived without self-isolating psychological separation, creates a comfort zone in which positive change is more likely to occur.

At ease, mentors. It is not necessary to experience non-dualism as your core reality in order to mentor non-dualistically. You need only understand the implications of the oneness of everyday reality and take a quantum leap to this truth: throughout our universe, everything that exists and everything that doesn't yet exist share the same Great Inventor Energy.

Mentors need not experience their day-to-day reality non-dualistically to have an awareness of the advantage of partnering with, celebrating, and harnessing Inventor Energy. Simply understanding that spirit is an ally in waiting will diminish the psychological distance between mentor and mentee.

Spirit's potential for helping us achieve our goals is so profound it is necessary to ask, 'How can we actualize spirit's potential?' We can do so by aligning ourselves with the power within, whatever its perceived source.

Is there evidence that a non-dualistic experience and holistic everyday expression of life can have a significant, positive effect on academic success? There is.

In his book, *Beyond the Post-Modern Mind*, Huston Smith writes that mid-way through the seventies, a grad student in psychology at New York University conducted an experiment to test a theory. He worked with a group of undergrads taking a six-week summer course in business law. The grad student divided his experiment's participants into two groups and before each class, for about a minute, he had them stare at a blank screen.

Four times during the minute, students in both groups saw a message flashed on the screen for so short a time that it was unseen in what appeared to be a flicker of light. Unknown to participants, the control group was subliminally imprinting 'People are walking.' The experiment group was subliminally imprinting 'Mommie and I are One.'

The outcome was notable. On the blindly marked final exam, the two groups, matched for GPAs, had different test scores. The 'Mommie and I are One' group averaged 90.4 percent, almost a letter grade higher than the control group, which averaged 82.7 percent.

The outcome of this experiment has been verified in eight studies. Regardless of the subject, positive results were achieved when messages connected the viewer of the screen to the cosmos and its life-giving spirit (154-155).

Mentors and mentees, talk about what spirit means to you and how you can draw upon your close-to-your-heart meanings for spirit as a powerful source of strength and inspiration. Discuss how you and they can connect with spirit, whether as a higher power, an instinct for survival (fire in the belly), or qualities of spirit. Regardless, spirit inspires high energy and sustained attention to a given task at hand, leading to achieved goals.

When a mentor reaches within for spirit and explains the process to a mentee, the inspired mentee will likely mirror the process (mirror neurons), which may help him find the inner and outer resources needed for success. The human spirit, regardless of its perceived source, helps generate self-actualizing direction and drive."

MIRROR NEURONS

"A striking example of spirit embracing all paths to itself is found in mirror neurons, discovered around 1990 in the lab of neuroscientist Giacomo Rizzolatti, at the University of Parma, Italy. What are mirror neurons? From www.wikipedia.com:

> 'Mirror neuron: a mirror neuron is a neuron which fires both when an animal performs an action and when the animal observes the same action performed by another (especially conspecific) animal. Thus, the neurons 'mirror' the behavior of another animal, as though the observer were himself performing the action. These neurons have been observed in primates, in some birds, and in humans. In humans, they have been found in Broca's area and the inferior parietal cortex of the brain. Some scientists consider mirror neurons one of the most important findings of neuroscience in the last decade.'

How do mirror neurons relate to mentoring? The neurons 'mirror' the behavior of another animal, as though the observer were himself performing the action. Ideally, a mentee will mirror his mentor's ways to be academically successful while living a satisfying social and spiritual life.

Mirror neurons research suggests that a key to learning rests with mimicking successful learning. If a mentee observes his mentor living a well-rounded, thriving life, mirror neurons in the mentee will imprint the successful model and, it is hoped, create a subconscious or conscious desire to imitate the learned behavior and actions leading to success.

Role rehearsals by mentors and mentees can foster mirror neuron mimicry. For example, a mentor, playing a teacher, can demonstrate how a teacher might react to a situation, played by a mentee. Role rehearsals by mentors and their supervisor can demonstrate suggested ways for mentors to handle difficult mentoring situations.

Mirror neurons are also thought by neuroscientists to be the center for developing empathy, and nothing in a mentoring relationship is more important than empathy."

START WHERE YOU ARE

"There are many paths to spirit's empowerment and revitalization. For some, their path is the guiding power of God or a higher power, whatever form or name it may take. For others, it is the dynamic human spirit inspiring them to work hard to achieve goals. Regardless, spirit can help a student triumph.

Dr. Bradford Keeney, renowned psychologist, wrote the following about how mentors and mentees can work with spirit to achieve their goals:

> 'Spirit, mystery, humility, play, and humor are all members of the same family. In their matrix, we find the direction we have been seeking, the intuitions that start us anew, and the creative inspiration that readies us for the next challenge. In spirit, we find the soulful life and the path worth living and dying for. I encourage you to reorient the way in which mystery rather than understanding, spirit rather than motivation, and love rather than reason can be the pillars of guidance in your everyday life.'

Thought provoking. 'Mystery rather than understanding.' Close your eyes and imagine where we are, in our galaxy, the Milky Way. Imagine beyond the three thousand stars we can see with unaided eyes. Imagine what you can of the hundreds of billions of stars spanning 80 billion trillion miles all around us. And that's just our galaxy. There are as many galaxies as there are stars in the Milky Way!

Imagine the beyond-mind miracle of it all and celebrate your own miracle, your life and all existence animated by spirit. In good conscience, can we do anything less than honor the miracle of existence by embracing and celebrating life's possibilities, especially education?

A cosmic perspective is beneficial when mentoring. Drum role for humility, please. The mystery of all of the above is deeply humbling and will awaken gratitude and aliveness in anyone who gets the big picture.

Indeed, mystery is more important than understanding. Human understanding and consciousness shape shift through the ages in response to limited levels of awareness and knowledge. Three hundred years ago people thought the universe was bound by a crystal sphere, with fixed stars twinkling in the night sky. The more mystery is understood, the more mysterious it becomes.

Mystery is all around us, in every life, distanced from the limited reach of our ego-based understandings. You never know where you are in your own story.

'Spirit rather than motivation.' I agree. Motivation is self-sustaining when it is a day-to-day expression of spirit.

No doubt about it—motivation without spirit is one dry biscuit. Desire without a flame is a weak motivator and often leads to academic inattention and academic probation.

When we live our life imbued with spirit, we live with our most powerful source of motivation, the life force within. Motivation that comes from outside one's self is usually less compelling. It lacks the personal meaning and commitment generated by the source of all.

Spirit is primal and uplifting. It elevates us to our higher nature and is renewable energy, unparalleled as a motivator.

'Love rather than reason.' When we are loved, we can do anything. When we are unloved, we become dispirited—without spirit. We may not feel like doing anything, especially schoolwork.

Lack of reason has caused far fewer sleepless nights than lack of love. Mentor with love (and with reason), understanding that the loving support mentees may have had at home is now probably far less available. Mentor in a loving way and you will fulfill a primary need—to love and be loved.

How can a mentor do this? By being the way we would like all humans to be—loving toward each other—relating through our common humanity, our vulnerability, our interdependence, the frailty and strength of the human family, Jews, Christians, Muslims, everyone, no exceptions.

Accessing and harnessing spirit is a daily goal most easily accomplished when we quiet our minds and thoughts. That is when spirit empowers our important goals and dreams, motivation quickens and success is possible. When we access spirit, we access clarity of mind and purpose. How we access spirit is a highly personal matter, but a calm, focused mind is best suited for the evocation. Feel out the situation. The way you, as mentor, present the possibilities for calling forth spirit is something you can decide as you get to know your mentees, if they are receptive.

Regardless of how you and your mentees conjure or summon spirit, an important goal should be the integration of spirit into daily life. Be open to conventional and unconventional means for flowing with the grain of life.

Students may align with spirit through, for example, meditation, yoga, prayer, mindful running or walking, drumming, chanting, breathing exercises, aerobics, and/or love, to name just a few. The inspiration and guidance of a higher power may also be found in nature, for me today, wildflowers, mountains in the distance, a circling hawk.

Breathing exercises are particularly well suited for students who want to draw forth spirit for strength and guidance, higher power or not. A breathing exercise can be done anywhere and is especially helpful in the minutes before beginning an exam. Strategically-timed breath work can help relieve stress and quiet the practitioner's mind, allowing for greater focus and insight. This is important because motivation and action to achieve goals are sparked through insight.

Regarding action, Eckhart Tolle wrote in *The Power of Now*, 'Action arising out of insight into what is required is more effective than action arising out of negativity (68).'

Breathing exercises quiet one's mind and can help reveal what is required."

[I will give each mentor one of Dr. Andrew Weil's CDs, *Breathing—The Master Key to Self Healing*, and ask that they teach one or two techniques to their mentees.]

Whatever form spirit takes, whether inspired by a higher power or the powerful human life force, bring spirit's guiding energy to each of your mentor/mentee relationships. Spirit, whatever its form, will deepen the reach of your mentoring."

SPIRIT CHECKLIST

Rate the last seven days from 1-5, with five as the highest rating. If you prefer, this can be a silent inventory. And remember, spirit means something different to everyone.

_____ How do you feel?

_____ How in touch are you with your spirit?

_____ How alive are you to the miracle of your own existence and all existence?

_____ How grateful are you for the opportunities you have?

_____ How hopeful are you?

Activity: Rate yourselves on the Spirit Checklist.

Discussion: What does spirit mean to you? How does spirit affect your daily life? How could spirit affect your life?

"A mentor recently wrote in a progress report: 'Thea liked rating herself daily on how she felt through mind, body and spirit, and these evaluations helped her see how she carried herself through the week.'

Everyone in the Student Peer Mentoring Program, minimally, should complete a Mind/Body/Spirit Checklist at the beginning of the semester, mid-semester, and the week before finals. Some will want to complete the checklists every week. Regardless, the focus areas of the checklist should be part of each week's mentoring discussion. Keep copies of all checklists and Seven-Day Plans in your binders for each mentee. And remember, this information is confidential. Use initials to identify your mentees."

[I will hand out copies of the checklists.]

CHAPTER SIX

Mentor Workshop Training

EMERGING INDEPENDENCE

This section of the workshop training focuses on the social aspects of college life.

"Regarding non-academic life, when students arrive at a college, all bets are off. They're free to present themselves any way they choose and their re-creation often leaves spirit at the gate. Without parents to control them, they discover who they think they might be, not who their parents think they are or should be. It may seem 'square' for a first year student to go to a place of worship.

As they transition from high school to college, students shed the strictures of their prior, more dependent life, and discover who they are by experimenting with possibilities. This is an essential part of their education and, with their consent, their choices should be discussed and reflected upon, not judged.

A mentee's decision to pursue or not pursue a relationship with their spirituality should be made without the slightest pressure from a mentor, even when a testing-the-possibilities personality emerges that threatens academic success. When that happens, mentoring questions can be more effective than mentoring warnings.

Bob Dylan sings, 'Reality has always had too many heads.' The social and academic disposition of entering freshmen is wide-ranging, from studious to 'Where's the party?', which can grab a disproportionate amount of a student's attention.

As you gently guide without judging, help your mentees keep social life in balance with academic life. Are your mentees making wise decisions? Resist the impulse to judge but do shine light on the paths they walk.

Heraclitus said that a person's character is his fate. Resist judging but be the changes you wish to see in your mentees. We want our program to have a positive impact on everyone's character. We want it to be uplifting, with a generosity of spirit that fosters academic, social, and spiritual well-being. To achieve this, we seek harmonious balance of mind, body and spirit, in ourselves and our mentees."

SHAPING THE MOMENT

"What do our mentees need? What are their hierarchies of the moment? What has shaped their attitudes toward education, relationships, sex, drugs, their health, their values, goals, and career aspirations? What makes them happy? What are their attachments and habits, their subconscious cultural and life scripts that determine their expectations and motivation?

The primal impulses of your mentees' psyches have been shaped by a money-worshiping culture that routinely measures self-worth by net worth. They have been culturally conditioned to want to make a lot of money so they can buy what they want when they want it, like right away.

Geography is often a key factor. Home for most college students is a significant distance away. Social support doesn't exist when they enter their dorm room, their new home. They arrive unknown to everyone at the college, and while this can be an unsettling reality it can also be an opportunity for a new life.

Since no one knows the student, what is to stop her from creating a successful academic and social life? No one knows if she has been considered a loser since kindergarten. No one knows the conclusions she has come to about herself, conclusions usually shared by dozens of people in her hometown community. If her conclusions bind her to a lack of self-confidence, she will suffer academically and socially."

THE RISK, THE POTENTIAL

"Adjusting to the unique culture and pressures of a college is quite challenging for all students. Not all do well. Some struggle with the adjustment and find themselves in crisis during their first semester. Crisis, as Chinese sages noted long ago, presents both opportunity and danger. The opportunity: getting a college education that will lead to a desirable life and career. The danger: falling flat on your face.

The opportunity of a college education includes a chance to learn to think independently and creatively, to develop a personal belief system, to examine and change biases and prejudices, to make conscious, well-intentioned choices. College life offers the opportunity to make new friends, fall in love, and attain knowledge, wisdom, self-discipline, self-confidence, self-esteem, a career path, and a life-altering education.

The danger for a student on academic probation is quite real. She is in danger of repeating attitudes and habits that contributed to her underachieving in the past. Her self-esteem may be low. Without needed support, she may get frustrated and not know whom to turn to and when. Without support, she may procrastinate with her schoolwork and that may be her undoing.

There is also danger that a first-year student will arrive at the college and her anonymity will make her feel invisible to her peers. Help her become visible, known to her classmates and teachers. When invisibility occurs, a mentee may feel emotionally distant and removed from everyone. Motivation and enthusiasm for school may slacken.

One of your many goals as mentors is to keep this from happening. You're going to help your mentees create balanced, visible college lives and identities, unless, of course, they prefer anonymity and invisibility. Help them get involved in their education. Encourage the perspective that learning is a golden opportunity. Only one person in one hundred on our planet goes to college."

KEEP ENERGY HIGH AND EMOTIONS POSITIVE

"This should be a day-to-day mantra for mentors and mentees: 'Keep energy high. Eat well, get enough sleep, exercise regularly. Keep emotions positive. Keep good company. Choose friends who support my success.'

Don't impose your own opinions, personal entanglements, or emotional needs on your mentees. Listen reflectively and hear them out. Listen with a full heart and a compassionate mind. Be present.

Mentoring should create a safe and expressive forum, a place and time for a mentee to discover, consider, and discuss her life as a student and ways to improve it."

SOCIETY'S MIRRORS

"The students you will be mentoring are similar in most respects to other first-year students. They arrive at the college with a belief system concerning life, love, and loyalty. They arrive believing in a self-image crafted over many years by their degree of success in high school, their extracurricular activities, peers dated or not dated, parental approval or disapproval. They arrive with preconceived beliefs regarding their relative attractiveness, intelligence, and desirability of personality.

They experience the miracle of existence with a culturally and socially acceptable degree of joy and gratitude, influenced by how much of their innocence and enthusiasm they've been able to retain through their teen years.

Mentors should pay particularly close attention to their mentees' projections of self. Through words, facial and verbal expressions, gestures, actions, and inactions, they will express their current life situation and expectations for themselves.

What are your mentees' aspirations? Their strengths? Weaknesses? Vulnerabilities? Habits and attachments? Have their values been shaped by spiritual leaders, community service, MTV, violent video games, or Internet pornography?

According to the U.S. Census Bureau's 'Statistical Abstract of the United States: 2007,' of the 3,518 hours Americans will spend next year with media, about half will be spent in front of a TV. About 146 days will be spent consuming media.

The mind mix of today's teenager includes thoughts of scarce jobs, suicide bombers, preemptive wars, and clashing civilizations. Your mentees, shaped by 9/11 and global terror, aren't sure they will have the economic opportunities and personal freedoms their parents and grandparents enjoyed.

No one knows for sure if a college degree will lead to a desired job. Belief that it will or won't can affect motivation, which is traditionally sustained by a belief that hard work will be rewarded by a high paying job. You and your mentees are society's mirrors. Pay attention to what you mirror and what is mirrored.

First-year college students form favorable or unfavorable opinions about their college in their first three to eight weeks. If they feel overwhelmed or alone, they're likely to form a negative opinion which may diminish their motivation and chance for success. That is why it is important to quickly form a good relationship with your mentees and encourage them to actively participate in what the college has to offer."

ON THE ALTAR OF
"I DON'T WANT TO BE ALONE"

"By the time students are college age, they've learned to craft desirable first acts, optimal ways of presenting themselves to others, motivated by a universal desire to be liked and accepted. To accomplish this, they project personalities that will increase the likelihood of acceptance and belonging. Unfortunately, first-act personalities are often like first dates—aimed to please and attract but incomplete presentations of self, lacking the more complex and less winning aspects of personality. This may result in your mentees' estrangement from important emotional and psychological needs of self. Authenticity is not infrequently sacrificed on the altar of 'I don't want to be alone.'

Especially during the first month of the semester, first-year students approach their peers with winning smiles and 'I'm one of you' banter, careful not to misplay a first impression, lest it be lasting. The drawback of introductory social masks is that they mask a student's need to be understood and accepted for who she is.

It is not uncommon for first-year students to avoid showcasing their less desirable characteristics when getting to know peers and faculty. They avoid saying or doing anything that will cause others to reject them. That's why early fall classes of first-year students are easiest to manage. Students are afraid to make waves or unnecessarily call attention to themselves. Knowing this, mentors should try to create mentor/mentee relationships that ring true and are close to the heart.

You, as mentor, may be the only one your mentee trusts enough to confide in. But take note: a mentor can only reach and share a mentee's inner life by authentically sharing some of her own. This builds the trust needed for Act II to make a comfortable appearance. Act II follows Act I: 'I'm a wonderful person, please like me.'

Act II reveals a person's shadow self, the aspects of self that raise eyebrows and disapproval, the act whose appearance we try to keep from public view. Act II is when we say and do things that turn people off. The sooner Act II can make a natural appearance, the sooner a mentee and mentor can work to lighten its impact.

The degree of social acceptance or isolation felt by a mentee may have a direct effect on her motivation and study habits. Mentors, tune in to these factors each week in your mentees and in yourselves as well. Are you and they living in optimal balance and harmony of mind, body and spirit?

Are you and/or your mentees wearing social masks when you meet? Do you share your time together honestly or do you keep each other psychologically at arm's length?"

WHO WAS THAT MASKED MAN?

"'Social masks?' you may think. 'So what if we wear them? Aren't they necessary? After all, the unseen masks we wear help us navigate the roles we play—son, daughter, student, staff, teacher.' True, but there is a down side to social masks, worn to give people what they expect will help them get what they want—a friend, a lover, a job, or a good grade. Social masks, however subtle and invisible, can easily lead to misunderstandings because of the emotional disconnect between what a person says and does, and what that person would like to say or do.

Any inauthentic interaction (sociopaths excepted) decreases a person's sense of peace, community, and well-being. We're nourished emotionally when we're able to express our feelings with honesty and trust to another human being.

First-year students arrive without a best friend and confidante. They don't have relationships that have been tested over the years. Peer mentors have the potential to create a safe haven for authenticity, where feelings can be shared in confidence.

Of course, if a mentee wants a more formal, less up-close relationship with her mentor, so be it, as long as the mentee is creating an effective Seven-Day Plan and participating actively in the program."

ROOMMATE WAR STORIES

"While many, if not most college dorm living situations are supportive, caring, and good company, over the years I have heard many intensely fought roommate war stories—cold wars, hot wars, wars of territory, wars over noise, drugs, sex, attitudes, over-socializing or social ostracism, slob behavior, smell behavior, taking someone else's food behavior, steal a girlfriend, steal a boyfriend, late night coughing, cell phone or Skyping behavior, to mention some of the most notable.

Mentors, you may have your own roommate war stories to share with your mentees if they're having problems. If you had problems, how did you handle them? Were you successful? With hindsight, what would you have done differently?

If a mentee is having roommate problems, talk with her about how she might best handle the situation. Perhaps a residence adviser or someone in housing would be the best person to intercede. The situation should be handled quickly, otherwise it can easily become a disabling distraction.

Students commonly give one-sided gripes about how insensitive and self-centered a roommate is. While the roommate may be a jerk, ask your embattled mentee if she is contributing anything to the difficulties. Is there anything she might do or say or discuss that would improve the situation? What is her ideal solution? Can someone mediate? Would finding another roommate or paying extra for a single dorm room be worth the money?"

THE JUICE OF GOSSIP

"The psychological and emotional dissonance caused by inauthenticity breeds a lack of trust that fosters insecurity. Lack of trust and insecurity spawn gossip, which races through a college like a successful virus, weakening trust and diminishing all involved. Gossip undermines by its very nature. It destabilizes its human target, inflicting discomfort for some, emotional trauma for others, sometimes even leading to suicide.

Though security is one of our most basic human needs, ironically, students who gossip to feel more secure are made less so by participating. Gossip undermines their security, making everyone potential prey. All students sense this.

The result is often free-floating anxiety and an ongoing echo-location of potential saboteurs of self-esteem. Thus the protection of cliques, a collective form of social self-defense.

Gossip is a habit of mind that distracts the mind, often to the point where a student finds it impossible to concentrate on schoolwork.

How can a student avoid gossip? By not gossiping, even passively, when others gossip. This isn't easy, given the tabloid quality of American life. Humans find dark pleasure in putting others down.

Talk to your mentees about the importance of not gossiping. Discuss the impact gossip can have on academic success. As soon as a student starts talking negatively about someone else, a chain of negativity is set in motion, weakening everyone involved. Gossip leaves mistrust and insecurity in its wake, distancing students from each other.

We're sensitive to others' perceptions of us, vulnerable to personality destabilization caused by social slights occurring in obvious and subtle, direct and indirect ways. A student shouldn't have to worry about whether people are talking about her behind her back, yet many students do worry and are hurt when they hear through the grapevine what another student has said about them. Their hurt may lead to depression, a weakened life force and low self-esteem. It is difficult to excel as a student when emotionally bruised.

Students enter college having grown up in a social and media world that uses gossip as a form of entertainment and a means of establishing controlling social norms. If your mentees have been the target of gossip, they may have developed a self-protective social posture, a twisted version of the golden rule: "Gossip about others before they gossip about you." If your mentees haven't been on the receiving end of cruelty and sarcasm, they surely know students who have.

Mentees may fear being ridiculed or rejected by others and may participate in gossip to avoid becoming a target of it. Gossip is a recreational sport. What students say and do, how they dress, their sexual and/or drug and alcohol preferences, are all grist for gossip mills that snake through college life. Gossip commands attention, tethering time to mind spinnings.

Gossip is a weapon used to hurt others, but sooner or later the weapon turns on the gossiper. Whatever goes around comes around. Gossiping about others all but guarantees that sooner or later, others will gossip about you. Hurtful social dramas caused by gossip can become time consuming distractions from a student's goal of succeeding academically; gossip is a habit of mind and tongue worth changing.

Doesn't everyone gossip? If mentees avoid people who gossip, won't they wind up spending most of their free time alone in their room? Not if they make a conscious effort to be friends with people who don't trade in the barbed side of human interactions. Positive people are out there—you just have to make a concerted effort to find them.

'Do you gossip?' Mentors should discuss this question with their mentees. The Student Peer Mentoring Program is holistic, designed to uplift mind, body, and spirit. Gossip can adversely affect all three. Negative talk and negative self-talk divert attention needed to achieve goals.

What effect does gossip have on spirituality? If we live our lives through our egos, as the vast majority of us do, gossip, ego's sidekick, distances us from our higher purpose, a spiritual purpose that can guide us, inspire us, and motivate us. A spiritual life, one that greatly diminishes the influence of ego, recognizes a higher purpose than social status among peers. A spiritual life reveres the gift of life and seeks to be a worthy expression of it."

FINDING FRIENDS, CHOOSING INFLUENCES

"Mentors can help mentees find new friends by creating a weekly goal of meeting at least three new students. Point out the importance of forming friendships with students who will support their efforts to succeed. Though the percentage of positive-thinking, hard-working students who will become friends is small, if the number is only one in twenty, your mentee will soon have a vital part of success in place: a social reason to be at the college.

Talk about the importance social life plays in doing well academically, and the importance of choosing friends who will respect their goal of a balanced life: mind/ body/spirit, and their dedicated effort to achieve each week's Seven-Day Plan.

The discussion mentors have with their mentees should include: What were your friends like in high school? How supportive were they? How compatible were their habits and values? What do you look for in a friend? How have your friends influenced you?

Discuss the effect friends can have on academic motivation and effort. A student recently told me she was withdrawing from college. 'I got in with the wrong crowd,' she said. 'Too much partying. I didn't pay attention to my schoolwork.'

Everyone needs someone to lean on and mentors may be that person until someone else comes along. Or you may be that person throughout your mentor/mentee relationship. Regardless, selecting supportive, academically-minded students for friends is important for mentees. The world is as you see it. If you're hanging out with friends who blow off schoolwork, you're more likely to do the same.

The new friends your mentees make will be influences, for better or worse. It is important to discuss the benefits of 'wise company,' as Buddha called it.

One area where new friends can exercise great influence is recreational drug and alcohol use. On any college campus a certain number of students will arrive with well-established drug and alcohol habits. They will look for friends with similar habits, seeking the party they've been to and enjoyed in the past. They will find students with habits they share.

It is easy for a student to fall in with a group that parties a lot and has a lackadaisical attitude toward schoolwork. This can affect a student's attitude toward her education and her desire to show up on time for classes. If needed, discuss the influence new friends can have on motivation and discipline.

Talk with your mentees about college clubs that will develop an interest and help them make new friends. The advantage of joining a club or two is that students in clubs have something important to them in common. They meet regularly and don't have to worry about being accepted or rejected by a group of peers. College clubs are a supportive social environment, almost always accepting of anyone who passionately shares the club's reason for being. The effort to create a good social life at the college should be weekly, deliberate, and selective."

ROMANCE, LOVE, EXPECTATIONS

"Do entering freshmen still long for Cupid's arrow to strike or is it all about hooking up and moving on? Some may arrive with hearts recovering from a high school romance turned hurtful. They may be wary of any relationship that could wound them deeply again, aware that it's rough out there. Hormones never learn.

Social needs may be more compelling than schoolwork. This reality is often a subtext of classroom discussions where half-listening minds sort through social yearnings, daydreams, possibilities and insecurities.

If discussion of social life is welcomed and relevant to academic success, make an appropriate place for it. If it isn't, let it be. It may take time before a mentee trusts enough to share social situations and circumstances affecting schoolwork."

CHOICES AND DECISIONS

"How conscious and deliberate are the choices and decisions we make? Are they well thought through and wise? Do we have a process we use, i.e., weighing the pros and cons, writing them down and contemplating them? Do we discuss difficult situations with a close friend, several friends, a parent, counselor, adviser, or mentor?

There are hundreds of choices and decisions that students make in the course of a week. They deliberate over some—'Should I ask her out?'—while they skate quickly over others—'What should I eat for lunch?'

The degree of deliberation over most choices and decisions falls somewhere in the middle. This may include whether to go to class, study or party, get high, or have sex. These are situations that may have significant repercussions for a mentee and her struggle to succeed. Reflective discussion of important choices and decisions before and after they're made is helpful, and may turn out to be an early stage of problem solving.

Discuss day-to-day choices and decisions that can negatively or positively affect your mentees' educations. Ideally, mentors will have relationships with their mentees that are close enough and trusting enough to provide a safe haven for discussions about personal and academic issues of importance that contribute to academic success and well-being.

While it should always be up to a mentee as to whether she wants guidance from her mentor regarding choices and decisions, mentees should know that mentors are available to help guide them, or to suggest someone who can help.

It is also important for mentors to understand that the parenting philosophies and styles of their parents will influence the choices and decisions they make as mentors. Some mentors will assert more authority and influence than others. Once the semester is underway, mentors should reflect on their mentoring styles and compare them with the way they were raised."

> **Activity:** Mentors will pair off with a mentor. Each will describe an educational situation where their self-esteem was diminished. That's how a mentee may feel being mentored by a fellow student.

Discussion: Talk about ways you can empower your mentees through the equality you share.

STRESS AND EMOTIONAL BALLAST

"A definition of 'ballast' in *Webster's New World Dictionary* is: 'anything giving stability and firmness to character, human relations, etc.' An effective way to reduce stress and have an enjoyable college life is by maintaining emotional ballast—equanimity.

Most humans live at the mercy of their emotions, which can easily turn stressors into stress. It is important for students to understand the influence stress and accompanying negative emotions can have on their ability to achieve academic goals. Feelings like fear, hate, jealousy, and depression can dominate, interfering with and overriding a stressed out student's ability to function effectively. This often leads to academic under-achievement.

The life of a student is continuously challenging and demanding, especially around midterms and finals when stress levels soar. Some students fall apart emotionally, succumbing to academic stressors by turning away from the dedicated study and preparation that is required. Some turn to binge drinking or excessive drug use. Others get lost in video games or texting. As for the Seven-Day Plan, later for that. Much later.

There are dozens of ways students yield to stressors, recoiling from the effort and courage it takes to meet college life challenges head on, day after day.

What is the ideal way to respond to stressors? Calmly. Dispassionately. With a steady gait and a steady mind; with equanimity. Ideally, students will not relate to stressors by ego-identifying with them. They, as humans, are not their situations. They do, however, have to deal with their situations, which are best handled proactively, wisely, with a sense of humor and an enjoyment of their 'one wild precious life.'

Situations come and go, even the ones that make a person feel like she's coming apart at the seams. A response to stressors via ego/identification commonly produces two counterproductive emotions—fear and anger. Neither is an ally for students.

High and low level stressors are part of every student's life but not all students get hyper-stressed because of them. Some are able to keep a light touch that doesn't disappear when the going gets rough. Some don't allow their minds to respond to stressors with a Pavlov-like triggering of emotions that are saboteurs of academic success. Minds that respond to stressors with untempered negative emotions are minds that have difficulty concentrating on schoolwork.

By example, mentors can help mentees learn how to temper their responses to stressors. Point out how you do it. Discuss how responding to stressors with some in-proportion anxiety is understandable and highly preferable to responding with paralyzing fear or hurtful anger.

One way, among many, to help your mentees keep perspective regarding their most undermining stressors is to ask, *What will happen if your worst fears become reality? What if you don't do well on an exam or paper? What if you do fail?*

Help your mentees keep perspective. There's nothing terminal about failure—humans are remarkably resilient—but why not avoid the comeback trail by walking the trail of the present moment? And why not walk it well?

Stressors abound in everyday life but they don't cause stress, they provoke it in those who allow their mind/body connection to be provoked.

Is stress having a negative effect on your mentees? Find out each week. Talk about their stressors, how they're responding to them, and how they might respond more effectively. Co-develop stress reduction programs that are part of your mentees' Seven-Day Plans. Discuss what works for them.

For college students, common stressors usually involve academic, interpersonal, or financial problems. Have they bought all books required for their classes? Are they looking for a part-time job? If they are, what are the possibilities? Can you help them?

Dorm life may be a fishbowl existence and/or a version of 'Animal House.' Most educational institutions of higher learning require dorm life for first year students, a year-long experience many students find stressful.

First-year students are assigned a roommate, and while some pairings are copacetic, as noted earlier, many are not. Most students are used to having their own bedroom at home. Now they not only have their own habits to contend with, they have the habits of a total stranger with whom they're sharing a room. Adapting skills are sorely tested, despite the best efforts of the college to match roommates according to academic and social compatibility. The results are often stressful.

College life is filled with daily stressors, any one of which can occupy thinking and work time. It is difficult to focus on schoolwork when everyday life interferes.

Be sensitive to your mentees' stress levels and their responses to stressors. Are they feeling overwhelmed, unable to do their schoolwork when they want to? If you think they are, let me know during our weekly meetings.

Seek optimum stress—enough to help motivate and achieve goals but not so much as to overwhelm or immobilize.

Are we living in more stressful times? We are. From the *Associated Press*, by Martha Irvine (01/11/2010):

'A new study has found that five times as many high school and college students are dealing with anxiety and other mental health issues as youth of the same age who were studies in the Great Depression era. The findings, culled from responses to a popular psychological questionnaire used as far back as 1938, confirm what counselors on campuses nationwide have long suspected as more students struggle with the stresses of school and life in general.

'It's another piece of the puzzle—that yes, this does seem to be a problem, that there are more young people who report anxiety and depression,' says Jean Twenge, a San Diego State University psychology professor and the study's lead author. 'The next question is: What do we do about it?'

'Though the study does not provide a definitive correlation, Twenge and mental health professionals speculate that a popular culture increasingly focused on the external—from wealth to looks and status—has contributed to the uptick in mental health issues.'

Sometimes a mentee will seemingly fall apart emotionally and will need more help than the mentoring program can provide. Mentors, if one of your mentees is slipping toward dysfunction, rage, or depression, discuss the situation immediately with me. And don't hesitate to talk about any mentoring situation that has become too emotionally demanding and/or inappropriate for a mentoring role.

To foster emotional ballast, which fosters academic achievement, encourage your mentees to practice their most effective means for quieting mind, exercising body, and enlivening spirit. Encourage them to build and use their network of support at the college, primarily you, me, supportive friends, the Academic Resource Center, advisers, faculty and staff. Make their network of support part of every Seven-Day Plan."

CHAPTER SEVEN

Mentor Workshop Training

THE HOME STRETCH

This conclusion to the workshop highlights the significance of peer and faculty support, and emphasizes empathy, organization, and other components of effective mentoring.

A CONSTELLATION OF MENTORS, A NETWORK OF SUPPORT

"Using available support will help your mentees achieve their potential, which will reduce their stress levels. Help them develop a cross-departmental and inter-institutional network of support among faculty, staff, and students, a constellation of mentors at the college who can support their efforts to be successful, mind, body, and spirit.

Who among family and friends back home should be part of their support, comfort, and guidance? A mentoring constellation can include mentoring experiences that are one time, every now and then, regularly scheduled, formal or informal."

SHOULD YOU BE FRIENDS?

"Sometimes a mentor/mentee friendship can enhance a mentoring relationship in an uplifting way. Sometimes a friendship can make it more difficult to mentor because mentee accountability may be awkward for the friendship. That can result in the mentor ignoring a pressing issue for fear he'll be seen by the mentee as parental.

Power-free mutual accountability is key. The mentor is accountable to the mentee for providing the help and guidance needed. The mentee is accountable to the mentor for providing active participation in the program. If a friendship undermines accountability, then friendship isn't in the best interest of mentee or mentor.

Whether friendship is beneficial to a mentor/mentee relationship depends on whether or not the friendship enhances or diminishes the success rate of accomplished goals each week. An honest appraisal is necessary before becoming friends with a mentee."

MENTOR WITH SOUL

"Bob Marley once sang, 'Only he who feels it knows it.' Experience and project empathy—feel what your mentees feel as they struggle to overcome their weaknesses and use their strengths to succeed.

Empathy is 'the recognition and understanding of the states of mind, beliefs, desires, and particularly, emotions of others. It is often characterized as the ability to put oneself into another's shoes, or experiencing the outlook or emotions of another being within oneself; a sort of emotional resonance' (www.wikipedia.com).

To develop empathy, which leads to trust, organically find emotional resonance with each of your mentees. You can do this by imagining yourself as someone with their life situation. Empathy and trust are cornerstones for effective mentoring, and when both are established, the likelihood of success increases significantly.

Is empathy an emotion and/or an experience? Research into mirror neurons suggests that empathy is both—an emotion and an experience. One reason for this may be that through mirror neurons we experience what another person is feeling, which develops empathy.

Perhaps mirror neurons are channels for spirit's oneness, allowing us to feel what another is feeling as if it were happening to us. It is a lot easier to walk in another person's shoes when they're your own shoes as well."

ACTIVE LISTENING IN THE PRESENT MOMENT

"It is common for students in a classroom to mentally multi-task, giving only partial listening attention to the subject at hand. While their professor lectures, or during classroom discussions, minds often wander to the past or future, actions taken or to be taken, desires, fears, hopes, conflicts. As mentors, model active listening in the present moment. Be an example of how to do it.

One of the most important teachings you can give mentees is how to listen attentively in a classroom, a dorm, anywhere. A student who tunes out what a teacher says because it is boring becomes prey for unrelated thoughts which compete for the student's attention and usually win.

Active listening helps keep competing thoughts at bay, for it is one-pointed, participatory listening. A student has to do more than just show up. He has to give his energy, focus, thoughts and responsiveness to the person or people talking.

Being fully present throughout a conversation or a teacher's lecture is an important form of participation. It requires respect for the speaker, which means the listener must mono-task, ignoring thoughts that distract. Focused listening in a classroom requires disciplined absorption in a subject, regardless of how uninspiring the information, point of view, or teaching style. This takes conscious awareness and practice.

The task we all have—threading a moving needle by being present."

THREE-RING ORGANIZATION

"I suggest the following organizational system for students: a three-ring binder with labeled sections for reading notes, returned papers, syllabi, class handouts, class notes, returned exams and quizzes. Some of your mentees will use a three-ring binder for each of their classes; some will use one binder for all classes, with tabs separating sections. They may want to tape their Seven-Day Plan to the inside cover of each binder."

[I will hand out three-ring notebooks for mentors and ask that they keep copies of their mentees' Seven-Day Plans in it, as well as comments about each mentee meeting and syllabi for each class. It is important that they bring their binder with them every time we meet in my office.]

"After you get to know your mentees, if you judge it appropriate, ask if they need any help organizing their dorm room. Can they find things easily?

Help them create a system of organization that balances the need for efficiency (wise use of time and effort) with the need to be comfortable with any self-imposed system of organization."

Discussion: What are your daily and weekly systems of organization? Describe why you use these systems, what makes them effective, and how you might improve them.

WHEN AND WHERE TO WORK ON ASSIGNMENTS

"It is important for your mentees to have a workspace they like and use regularly. It should be well-lit, quiet, and free from distractions. A mentee's Seven-Day Plan should include where he will study, and when. Discuss the advantages and necessity of a workspace conducive to achieving goals. Once a mentee associates a study area with accomplishing objectives, the positive association will increase the likelihood of success every time the workspace is used.

A study area should not be accessible to friends, unless they are serious and effective study partners. A secluded corner of the library is often ideal. A shared dorm room usually is not. Interruptions and distractions are more likely in a dorm room and a bed is too close to ignore when a mentee gets bored or tired.

Are study partners a good idea? Sometimes. Students culturally wired for entertainment and digital distractions may have a difficult time working alone on their assignments. They may need the company of another student. This can work if the company is dedicated to academics. If the partnering turns into a social get together, suggest that your mentees do their studying, reading, researching and writing papers either alone or with someone else.

When is the best time to do schoolwork? This is an important question and your mentees' answers should be used when co-creating their Seven-Day Plans. How do you determine the best time to study? By tuning in to levels of energy and alertness at different times of the day and night. Those interested in exploring the subject in greater depth can investigate biorhythms."

BREAKING WITHOUT BRAKING

"When studying, mentees should pace themselves, taking breaks when needed and deserved. How often is that? Often enough and short enough so they are able to get back into their academic work without a loss of interest, concentration, or momentum. They should take a break primarily to sustain the effectiveness of their study time. A secondary reason is as a reward for doing what they should have been doing anyway. But note if the 'reward' break turns out to be longer than the 'clear your head and get back to work' break.

Should a break be ten minutes or thirty? That depends on the psychological and neurological makeup of a student and how long the student has been studying. Given the short attention spans that have been hard-wired into humans through texting, tweeting, and mass media sound bites, the length of a study break is highly personal. Students with ADD or ADHD will need more frequent breaks and should consider having malleable toys they can manipulate to help dissipate stress and minimize susceptibility to distractions."

A FEW BASICS BUNDLED

"You will meet with your mentees at mutually agreed upon times and places. Fogolson Library is a good meeting spot but you can meet anywhere, as long as it's conducive to uninterrupted mentoring.

During your meetings, go over syllabi for each of their classes. Make sure they're starting assignments early enough, with specific dates for drafts of papers. Help them stay motivated and on task. Are they keeping up with their schoolwork? Preparing well for their tests? Ask them. Did they get any grades or papers returned?

With their permission, keep track of all grades they receive, their general state of well-being, and obstacles they're encountering. Recognize and be happy for each of their successes, no matter how small they seem. Positive reinforcement works!

As you become aware of your mentees' academic and social self-beliefs, help them change any behaviors that undermine their potential as students: procrastination, passivity, un-engaged listening in class, self-sabotage, poor self-esteem, undermining self-talk, risky drug/alcohol use, debilitating stress, disorganization, lack of motivation, ineffective management of time, unwise choices, self-isolation, partying too much, or not enough sleep, exercise, and/or regular meals that nourish."

UNWRAPPING YOUR GIFT

"We work every day with the basic hand we were dealt at birth. How well we work with our hand is key to whether we achieve our goals. Consider your "hand" your greatest gift. Most people never fully unwrap their gift because they're too afraid to see their own limitations and weaknesses—too hard on the ego. Transformation of negative habits is within reach of everyone but it requires great honesty and effort.

Setting goals and meeting them every week while strengthening learning and study skills creates momentum for positive transformation. When a student makes a continuous practice of good mind/body/spirit habits, potential is actualized.

The means for unwrapping your gift is self-knowledge, the human tap root for motivation and positive change. Lasting transformation occurs when a person fully unwraps his or her greatest gift, himself, herself, and says, 'OK—let's get to work.' Be the world you want to live in. Mentor that world."

FARE THEE WELL: END OF MENTOR WORKSHOP TRAINING

[I will give mentors the names and phone numbers of their mentees and their mentees' responses to the questions in the academic probation letter I sent them (*see Chapter Two*).]

"Our workshop training has now come to an end and I pronounce you all 'mentors.' Your training will continue each week when we meet individually in my office, and when we meet once a month as a group. We'll set up meeting times. If you want to discuss something right away, call me or stop by my office. Fare thee well, mentors."

CHAPTER EIGHT

Continue to Train Mentors throughout the Semester and Evaluate the Program

When I meet with a mentor for a half hour each week to discuss their mentoring, we begin by talking briefly but personally about what's going on in their life, thereby developing *our* relationship. Then we talk about their mentees and the progress they're making or not making.

At various times I ask to see copies of their mentees' class syllabi, Seven-Day Plans, the results of their Learning and Study Strategies Inventories, and their Mind/Body/Spirit Checklists. We discuss each mentee's developing network of support, their goals, challenges, and actions they are taking to achieve their goals. For each mentor, I maintain a folder containing my notes on their mentees, drawn from our weekly meetings.

We brainstorm ways to help bring their mentees into more complete holistic balance. Our meetings are spirited, the way I want their mentoring to be.

On occasion, when a mentoring situation warrants it, I meet with a mentor and mentee together. On rarer occasion, I meet with a mentor, a mentee, and one of the mentee's professors to discuss how we can work together to help the mentee pass the professor's class.

Once a month I meet with mentors as a group. At noon, we gather at a table in a private room and over lunch, usually pizza and cold drinks, we discuss mentoring.

Without revealing the identities or identifiable challenges of mentees we are discussing, mentors share and explore mentoring situations, what's working and what isn't, with suggestions offered in a relaxed, supportive environment. These meetings are a continuation of my mentor workshop training. I am a guiding teacher and facilitator, encouraging them to learn from me and from each other.

HOW ARE WE DOING?

The week after midterms each semester, I have mentors give their mentees the following evaluation questions:

- How would you describe your relationship with your mentor?
- How has your mentor helped you succeed academically?
- How has your mentor helped you balance the academic, social and spiritual aspects of your life?
- Which learning and study skills are you working on with your mentor?
- What are your suggestions for how your mentor could be more effective when mentoring you?

I also ask mentors to respond to these questions:

- What do you like and what do you not like about mentoring in the college's Student Peer Mentoring Program?
- What are your suggestions for improving the program?

When I next meet with mentors individually, we review their mentees' evaluation comments as well as their own. We discuss what would improve their mentoring and the mentoring program.

The week before the semester ends, I ask mentors to write a paragraph about their overall impression of the Student Peer Mentoring Program. I ask mentors to have their mentees do the same.

I keep my evaluations simple. Other programs may want more complex evaluations than I use. Rey Carr writes the following about evaluations: "An evaluation method to consider is the four-level model. Most mentoring programs or services are concerned about some type of evaluation. But often the method chosen to conduct the evaluation only measures a small portion of what occurs as a result of their mentoring strategy."

In an effort to create a systematic approach to evaluation that would provide more powerful information, Donald Kirkpatrick created in 1975 a model that has now become known as the Kirkpatrick Model or the Four-Level Evaluation Model. This model is easy to understand and apply and allows for great diversity:

Level 1—REACTION
This is probably the most commonly used element of this model. Here the goal is to evaluate the reactions of participants to a training program. Questions are posed to the participants at the completion of the program regarding their feelings, thoughts, ideas, or opinions of what they just experienced. This level is sometimes called the "smiley face" or "happy face" level of assessment. This description should not be used to think of this level as being worthless or any less important than the other three levels. For example, this level of evaluation can provide valuable information about the relevance of training objectives, the degree to which participants maintained interest in the training, the participant's experience of the amount of time or types of course interaction, and the participants' perceived value of the ways in which the training will be of value to them for some future or ongoing activity.

This is probably the most popular form of evaluation because it is relatively easy and inexpensive to administer.

Level 2—LEARNING RESULTS
What did the participants actually learn? What impact did the training have on the participants in terms of their skills, knowledge and attitude? At this level, participants are asked about what they actually learned. It may turn out there is a gap between what the participants really learned and what the course designers had expected them to learn. In this type of evaluation, there is a close match between the content of the questions asked of participants and the content of the learning objectives for the course or training.

This is also a commonly used approach and often is demonstrated through a pre- and post-assessment instrument.

Level 3—BEHAVIOR

Here the focus is on the degree to which participant learning is applied in the real world (i.e., workplace, school environment, etc.). In essence, are the participants able to put into practice what they learned in the initial training? Is what they learned being transferred? And is the learning maintained over time or does it have a fatigue or drop off? Is there a match between what the peer mentors learned to do in their training and what they actually do when interacting with their peer mentor partners?

While there is often a strong desire to learn about "on the job" transfer of learning, it receives less attention because it often requires follow up from three to six months after the initial training has been completed or is best determined through actual observations or supervisory reporting. In addition, contacting the people who interact with the peer mentor to determine the impact can require some creative ways to deal with confidentiality and tracking.

Level 4—RESULTS

At this level the goal is to determine what impact the training/course has on the organization. Did the training add to the value/vision/ mission of the organization? What changes in productivity and results were observed in the organization? Return on investment (ROI) measures would fall here.

This level might appear to be more complex to assess because many factors (in addition to or possibly even in conflict with the training/ course) can contribute to the growth of the organization. However, anecdotal information or data normally collected as part of the operation of the organization can be useful. For example, overall grade point average, dropout or retention rates, completion of studies rates, visits to crisis center, use of tutoring, and such could be measures relevant to the impact of peer mentoring on the organization resources. Note that either an increase or decrease in visits to a crisis center could indicate the value of a peer mentoring service.

One of the best resources for learning more about this model is at www.businessballs.com/kirkpatricklearningevaluationmodel.htm.

ADDITIONAL EVALUATIONS

After mentors know their mentees' midterm grades, I ask mentors to write a progress report for me about each of them. After writing their grades to date, and what learning and/or study strategies they have been working on and will be working on for the second half of the semester, mentors write a general assessment of their mentees. Here are two examples of these progress reports:

> **ELLA** is doing fine overall, but is behind on one paper. She has been in contact with her teacher about the reasons why. Ella says she has been having intense feelings of anxiety (she says that all aspects of her life have been really hard to deal with—familial, social, and academics). I am worried about her. We plan to meet more than the allotted hour, and I'm going to remind her of the study sessions on Sunday. She is having difficulty keeping the different parts of her life separate from one another and I think more frequent meetings will benefit her.

[This mid-semester progress report caused me to set up a meeting with mentor and mentee to develop a plan to improve Ella's situation.]

> **AARON** is a sophomore who was in the mentoring program last year. He is on academic probation until he brings his GPA above a 2.0. Last semester, Aaron came close but did not quite make it.

Challenges last year:
- not going to class
- getting to sleep late
- not very awake in class
- not showing up for mentoring meetings
- resistance to get tutoring help with his writing

Progress:
- class attendance has been virtually perfect
- not staying up late as before, getting better sleep
- more alert in class
- has shown up for all of his mentoring meetings this semester

- has come to understand that tutoring is not just for last minute assignment execution, but for general skill development
- has warmed up to the idea of making a countdown of days on his planner until due dates of major projects
- has also warmed up to the idea of breaking larger projects into smaller, more manageable tasks (for example, a 20-page paper, one page a day for 20 days)
- writing skills are improving

Midterm grades:

Art History II—B

Mixed Media—B

Clothing as Metaphor—B

Main concerns:

- Aaron is still not independently vigilant about looking at his syllabi and planning accordingly
- He may benefit from understanding that his body language and lack of communication could give people the impression he does not care

Prognosis:

Aaron seems to be on track to get off academic probation this semester.

Evaluating a student peer mentoring program should include a statistics-based look at persistence and retention. Have the students in my peer mentoring program persisted and been retained by the college as a result of the mentoring program? They have. Have their grades improved? Consistently. The mentoring program has served more than one hundred students over five years. The GPAs of 86.2 percent of them improved while they were in the program and thereafter. The average GPA for students after a semester in the program was 2.66, a notable achievement considering their high risk when they entered the program.

I'm pleased with how effective the program has been and the academic success of our mentees. Most have stayed in the program for a semester and after getting off academic probation have continued to do well on their own, meeting with me on occasion, as well as staff and tutors at the Academic Resource Center. After they leave the program they continue to seek out and work with a constellation of short-session mentors throughout the college. Mentees' grades have improved, as have their retention rates.

I've had mentees who stayed in the program with the same mentor for a year and as long as two years. Most stay in the program one semester and achieve one of the program's goals: self-directed self-mentoring.

CHAPTER NINE

Mentoring Crises and Disabilities

A STORY FROM THE FRONT: PAUL'S RETURN

Most mentoring is challenging but manageable, sometimes frustrating, but far more often very satisfying. It is a valuable experience for mentees and their mentors. In rare instances, however, the psychological/emotional state of a mentee becomes so extreme that a mentor is not the right person to take on primary responsibility for the mentee's well-being. That job should fall to the program's supervisor, initially, and then whoever the supervisor thinks can best be at the helm of decision making regarding the student in crisis. No one is immune to being overthrown by the heartache of the human condition, including mentors. Paul's story illustrates this.

Each year, I have a pool of dependable, excellent students to draw upon—students who have mentored or want to mentor. Every supervisor needs such a list to build their program from year to year, students safe and steady enough to mentor. Paul was one of these students. I could match him up with anyone. Largely because of his own struggles as a student, he had a compassionate, easy way of working with peers who had years of their own struggles and setbacks. For two years at the college he was a well-liked, successful student. Then his world turned up-side-down and he fragmented psychologically, unable to function academically or socially.

With permission from Paul, and identifiable specifics of his story changed, here is an illuminating tale.

Paul is a junior. He is an achieving student, a mentor, student ambassador, and representative in student government. As a junior in high school he learned techniques and strategies for dealing with his

ADHD, and he is brilliant at sharing his knowledge and experience with the students he mentors. He and his girlfriend, dating for two years, are talking about getting married after they graduate. Then Paul's world implodes. The summer before his senior year, his girlfriend meets someone at a music workshop, falls in love, and transfers to a college near him. Paul is devastated.

WHEN THE WINDS OF CHANGE SHIFT

Paul returns for the Fall semester and I welcome him back to the mentoring program as a highly valued and effective mentor. But the first time I see him, the third week in August, it is apparent he's having difficulty coping with routine challenges of everyday life. His affect is flat, he doesn't make eye contact and he appears shaken, depressed to his very soul.

I ask if he's all right and he says no, he's broken up with his girlfriend, he's using drugs and alcohol but doesn't want to talk about any of it. I ask if he thinks it would be a good idea to see a mental health counselor and he says he'll talk to someone at the Wellness Center. He adds, "I'm not in any condition to mentor this semester." Clearly, he isn't. I ask if he would like to be mentored by Richard, someone Paul knew from our monthly mentor meetings the previous year. He says yes.

I call Richard, who had gotten too busy to continue mentoring this fall. With confidentiality assured, I describe Paul's condition and ask if he could find time to mentor him. Richard says yes and agrees to meet Paul in my office the following afternoon.

About Richard—everybody likes him. He's from an Hispanic family living in Espanola, New Mexico, a Moving Image Arts major, going to college full time and working fifteen hours a week as a waiter for an upscale restaurant.

MANAGING PAUL'S CRISIS

The next day, waiting for Richard in my office, I ask Paul if he talked with anyone at the counseling center. Withdrawn and nervous, he shakes his head no and says he didn't go.

Richard comes in with his reassuring presence and we all shake hands. I tell them I have a few things to do and as I close the door I hear Richard say, "How you doing, man?"

The semester begins. I meet with mentors and mentees, my office is filled with students coming and going, everybody making adjustments to the new semester.

Before the end of the semester's first week, Richard tells me "Paul didn't show for our meeting and didn't respond to voice mail messages. I went to his dorm room, knocked on the door; he called out for me to come in. Turns out he's so depressed he can't even get out of bed. He refuses to see a counselor. I set up a morning routine for him and a time to go to bed. He says he's willing to try, but he's in really bad shape."

"I know his residence adviser. I'll call him and ask that he look in on Paul."

I do so after Richard leaves, and I alert the dean.

CIRCLES OF RESPONSIBILITY AND INFLUENCE

After talking with Richard, it becomes clear that Paul needs more help than Richard and I and his residence adviser and the dean can provide. I tell Paul's story because boundaries of responsibility and influence are important issues for supervisors and mentors to assess when a mentee (or a former mentor) is in crisis. As supervisor, it was up to me to quickly co-develop a network of primary support that would provide the help Paul needed.

His story illustrates the importance of boundaries, targeted responsibilities, and knowing whether you're inside a circle of responsibility and influence or outside it. Understanding the difference is vital to effective, ethical, liability-free mentoring and mentoring programs. Program supervisors have a responsibility to make sure their mentors don't take on a therapy/counseling role with their mentees.

When a student is in crisis, regardless of how skilled a mentor may be, supervisors, not mentors, are in charge of making sure the student immediately gets needed help. To ensure this, program supervisors, encourage your mentors to discuss with you any mentee who is having difficulty coping. Follow up by meeting with the troubled mentee. Assess his situation and decide what support is needed short-term, and who will provide it. Then make it happen.

As program supervisor, take charge of the well-being of a student in crisis until you find someone in a more appropriate circle of responsibility and influence to be the point person. Continue to provide consultative support if requested, as well as ongoing mentoring support.

Paul refuses to see a mental health counselor at the college, but signs a release allowing me to talk with his mother. She turns out to be the point person. In the weeks that follow, she monitors his situation from Boston through our phone conversations at least once a week and makes decisions regarding his care. She is the appropriate circle of responsibility and influence.

But as weeks pass with little improvement to show for the support Paul is receiving, his mother talks with me about withdrawing him from the college and flying him home to Boston if he doesn't start going to all his classes and doing the work. She says she's going to tell him this and follow through if he doesn't agree to see a college counselor or a local therapist in town. She asks me to meet with him.

When I meet with Paul in my office, he avoids eye contact. I ask how he is. He says, "The same." My tone is supportive. "I spoke with your mom the other day. She asked if you were going to your classes. I told her some of them, not all of them. She said she was going to withdraw you from the college if you don't see a therapist in Santa Fe and get back into your schoolwork. She said she was going to talk with you and tell you."

He shrugs. "Maybe it would be best for me to go home and see someone in Boston."

"That's one possibility. Another is you see a good therapist in Santa Fe, finish the semester, and graduate in May."

"I don't know. I'm a loser here. I feel worthless."

"Worthless? Where did that come from? I hear from students all the time what a great guy you are." He looks at me and I continue: "You need to change your self-perception. I know your heart is broken and it hurts beyond all description, but that's your situation, it's not you.

"Healing will take time but it will happen. The choice is yours. You can continue to see yourself as defeated, a failure, or you can see yourself as the really good person you are, healing from a painful breakup, someone who has helped many students, someone smart and talented with a great future as a teacher. You can live your life with gratitude—now there's worth. And here's some more. Let me read you what Will wrote about you as his mentor:

'I'm back at the college because of one person, my mentor, Paul. He never gave up on me, even after I had given up on myself. He always believed in me. I can't say that about too many people in my life.

'Paul believed in me and gave me the tools to survive as a student at the college. He knew what I needed better than I did and he taught me the skills that have made him successful. He's an amazing teacher, a really great human being. When he teaches something, or inspires me, it has impact that stays with me. I've changed because of him. My grades have improved. I'm off academic probation. I'm a better person.'"

Tears well up in Paul's eyes. "That's me," he says, stunned by his recognition of a former self he really liked and respected.

"That's you," I say. "You're going through a difficult time right now but you'll get through it. You're the guy Will wrote about."

Something shifts in Paul. He stops by the college wellness center and gets a referral to a highly regarded local therapist. His psychological improvement is incremental in the weeks that follow. His depression and apathy lift by degrees, enough so he passes all his classes, though barely. An extremely difficult mentoring situation comes to a successful end. Again: nothing initiates change more powerfully than a revised self-image.

TALK ABOUT IT

During your weekly supervisory meetings with mentors, ask if they're having a difficult time dealing with the emotional/psychological state and needs of any of their mentees.

Sometimes we can mentor others but we can't mentor ourselves. There are times when the ground under our feet disappears and we handle the trauma through one pain management addiction or another.

Sometimes we can mentor others but we can't access for ourselves what others access in us. We can't give ourselves the gift we give others. We can't find a thriving balance of mind, body, and spirit on behalf of our own potential.

There are times when humans succumb to contracted states of consciousness that manifest as mental illness, depression, and/or other states of being that separate them from spirit. Once these states are healed or transcended, the human channel for spirit is re-established and it can once again guide from within. Paul knew he needed spirit to mentor effectively and when his state became inaccessible to spirit, he resigned as a mentor.

When we mentor, we mentor states of consciousness. Unfortunately, a person's state of being is sometimes so dark as to not allow any light in.

THE DISABILITY AND ABILITY OF LOVE

With one exception, the names and personally identifiable academic and social situations of mentors and mentees in this book have been changed to protect and encourage free expression of valuable lessons learned. The one exception is Keith Murfee. Keith was in the mentoring program for a semester and I've worked with him for more than two years as his mentor. He is a talented writer and musician whose courage and self-advocacy are inspiring.

Born with cerebral palsy and judged different throughout his 25 years because of a slight speech impediment, it is hard to know if Keith has suffered more from his physical infirmities, or from the cruel taunts and bullying of classmates, kindergarten through college. This remarkable young man has the mettle to bring his knowledge out into the light so it can be examined, and he can be healed, and he can help heal others with his wisdom expressed through his writing.

I excerpt from a sermon Keith wrote and gave at his church in Washington, DC.

> "Having a disability is challenging but it shouldn't lead to a depressed life. However, it often does because of the mindset people without disabilities have towards people with them.
>
> "A friend and mentor, Scott Seldin, suggested I write a piece entitled 'The Disability of Love.' I was intrigued by the concept. We all have a disability, whether we know it or not, accept it or reject it. It is the need for love. The lack of awareness we bring to our inability to love is the disability that haunts us all. It is the common ground of life."

This is an important insight to have when mentoring, whether or not your mentee has a documented disability. Step into the world of your mentees as you step more deeply into your own world. Is your limited ability to love turning those with documented disabilities into "other?"

Henry Thoreau once wrote, "Dreams are the touchstones of our character." Keith fights every day to keep his dreams alive, which means keeping alive his ability to love and be loved.

Working on a dream with elevated consciousness requires loving effort every day, in class and out. It requires finding support on campus and off, and recognizing that support may include places of worship and/ or meditation. These centers can give students clarity of purpose and an awareness of how to live life for its highest good.

MAINTAINING THE SACRED

When students leave home for college, they leave behind their network of support, which usually includes almost everyone who loves them. And everyone they love. For some, their loss includes their place of worship, prayer, and/or meditation. It is important to recognize the regenerative, supportive role a spiritual center may have played in a first-year student's life before starting college.

It is also important to recognize what the loss of a spiritual practice can mean for students who drew strength and purpose from time set aside each week for the sacred.

Every year, for several students, the most valuable help I give is re-connecting them with their spiritual path in their new home, helping them find a home for their spiritual practice. If a student expresses interest, I offer a pamphlet of local religious and spiritual centers. Most cities and communities have similar community directories available for anyone who asks.

SOURCES OF STRENGTH AND INSPIRATION

Of course, your mentees' sources of strength and inspiration may be sources that are separate from spirit's centers of worship and/or meditation. If so, don't abandon spirit, for it thrives in secular life as well. Just take a look around at the miracle of your own life. Call it Ishmael, it's still spirit, and should embody every mentoring meeting.

During my fifteen years as a composition and literature teacher at Baruch College, the exceptional and highly respected business school located in the heart of Manhattan, I experienced the indomitable spirit of

Baruch's thousands of urban students. They drew spirited strength from self-knowledge gained from living in the city.

The diversity of students at Baruch contributed to multiple world perspectives in every class, resulting in a depth of educational and social experiences for all students, faculty, and staff. Students were from all over the world, providing each other an extraordinary educational resource, just from being together.

I made the richness of their cultures part of every class. I asked who their heroes were and those were the authors we read, including Nikki Giovanni, Langston Hughes, Richard Wright, and lastly, James Baldwin, their favorite. We poured over his book, *The Fire Next Time*, and the papers they wrote were some of the most brilliant I've ever read. They expressed their sources of strength and inspiration in the face of overwhelming odds.

Learning about their lives deepened my own, inspiring me as the great writers we read inspired them. And when we were fortunate enough to receive the inspiring figure of James Baldwin as guest speaker, everyone stood up and cheered like he was a rock star.

CHAPTER TEN

In Community—
Santa Fe and Northern New Mexico

To provide a model for creating a mentoring program with a keen sense of its historical and current place in its community, I offer my own sense of place, living in northern New Mexico, working at the College of Santa Fe. The Student Peer Mentoring Program I created was shaped with the college's culture, history, and mission in mind, as well as the cultures, histories, and geophysical influence of the environment, in this case, Santa Fe and northern New Mexico. D. H. Lawrence once said of New Mexico, "Touch the country and you will never be the same again."

Your school's students will have their own individual and collective histories and stories that will be reflected in your program's character, goals, and ways of integrating spirit into everyday life. Create your program with a free, spirited hand.

ABOUT THE COLLEGE

Located at 7,000 feet above sea level in the foothills of New Mexico's Sangre de Cristo Mountains, the arts are central to the College of Santa Fe. Students are drawn to the college by its reputation for exceptionally good programs in art, graphic design, moving image arts, photography, creative writing, and performing arts.

The environment at the college is informal, relaxed, and project-oriented. Many in the student body who were outsiders in high school experience themselves as insiders for the first time.

Faculty are usually working artists, inspiring, knowledgeable teachers who encourage creative freedom and collaboration, using the college's small size for frequent one-on-one faculty/student meetings. Comprehensive student support is readily available.

The intention of my positive characterization of the College of Santa Fe is to give the reader an accurate portrait of the home of the Student Peer Mentoring Program I designed for the college.

The origin of the College of Santa Fe is a tale straight out of the Old West. In 1859, at the request of Reverend J. B. Lamy, first bishop of New Mexico, four Christian Brothers left France and headed for Santa Fe, traveling two months along the Santa Fe Trail by train, horseback, and wagon, to create a school for boys in Santa Fe. The school, St. Michael's College, opened December 15, 1859. The classroom the Brothers used was an adobe hut near the oldest church on the Pecos Trail.

WE'RE NOT IN KANSAS ANYMORE

An educational experience takes place in a community, a neighborhood, a place with an important history and character. Learning is enriched when it draws on the human and institutional resources of its community.

Consider what it might mean to go to college in the "City Different." Life *is* different here. I've heard students say that living in northern New Mexico is like living in another country—it's that different. When someone from New Mexico tried to buy tickets to the 1996 Olympics in Atlanta, Georgia, he was told they were only selling tickets within the United States!

New Mexico is an unpopulated state, second to Mississippi as poorest, and when students arrive from almost anywhere else, they experience culture shock and have considerable adjusting to do.

For many, the adjustment begins with Santa Fe's high altitude. Low-altitude lungs don't know what happened to all the oxygen they used to breathe. Arriving students are told to drink plenty of liquids, especially during their first month here. Good advice.

Another adjustment—everywhere they look, students see adobe houses and buildings, the required architecture of Santa Fe. Adobe, originally baked mud and straw, now often faux adobe, is central to the aesthetic and consciousness of the City Different. With all the buildings earth-toned, the human ego is less dominant on the beautiful high desert landscape.

Students also have to adjust to the ways the three most populous cultures living in Santa Fe and northern New Mexico, Native, Hispanic, and Anglo, interact and live in community. Native tribes have been here for thousands of years—Hispanics and Anglos for many hundreds of years. Their entwined, highly charged histories continue to play out in everyday Santa Fe, giving students an opportunity to enrich their educations by learning about the communities, traditions, beliefs, and histories of the people of this region, where the past is ever present.

In his book, *Santa Fe Hispanic Culture: Preserving Identity in a Tourist Town*, Dr. Andrew Lovato writes about how the Spanish created the "encomienda" system during their colonization of New Mexico:

> "This arrangement required Pueblo Indians to provide basic provisions to the Spaniards such as food and blankets in exchange for Christian education and protection. This system put a great deal of strain on the pueblos, especially during times of drought and because of the dwindling Indian population, due in part to diseases such as smallpox and influenza introduced by the Spanish . . . . By 1680, half of all Spanish households owned slaves, with many having multiple Indian servants.
>
> "Sixteen-eighty was the year Po'pay, an Indian leader, warrior, and farmer, gathered various tribes and led a successful revolt that forced 1,000 Spanish settlers to flee to El Paso. The settlers returned several years later and Santa Fe celebrates their return and 'resettlement' with a Fiesta."

Lovato continues:

> "Perhaps the single event that did the most to change the nature of the territory was the coming of the railroad in 1880. New people arrived by the thousands. Between 1880 and 1900, the Anglo population of New Mexico quadrupled. By 1886 Spanish-surnamed property ownership diminished by 48 percent.
>
> "A new elite comprising Anglo lawyers and territorial government officials developed in Santa Fe. This informal coalition, which has been referred to as 'The Santa Fe Ring,' appropriated vast amounts of land during the late 1880s and early 1900s. By 1912, it had manipulated the judicial and legislative systems to such an extent that it controlled 80 percent of the former lands held by Mexican farmers and ranchers" (10-12).

What is the relevance of this history to the Student Peer Mentoring Program at the College of Santa Fe? Understanding the present historical and sociological moment helps out-of-state students feel more comfortable in their new home. A student reading Andrew Lovato's historical account would better be able to understand, interact with, and learn from the various cultures of northern New Mexico.

The mentoring program I created for the College of Santa Fe was responsive to the college's character and history, and the history of Santa Fe. It is my hope that the brief background information I have given will suggest a process the reader might use to create a mentoring program tailored to their school of interest, its town or city's history, and the school's place in the community. Recognizing this honored position is important for any mentoring program. Our digital/cyber age has remarkably shallow roots and as a consequence, little sense of place. (Where exactly *is* cyber space, anyway?)

A sense of place helps ground students, especially those far from home, orienting them to unfamiliar surroundings, people, cultures, and institutional expectations. Adjusting to place facilitates quicker transition time from "somewhat dazed new student," to "focused, achieving, and enjoying life new student." Somewhat dazed new students tend to hide out in their culturally familiar, techno-world. Mentors can help mentees adjust to their new surroundings. Share your favorite stamping grounds and activities, and encourage your mentees to learn about and experience their new community's diverse cultures.

JOSEPH IS NATIVE

The importance of creating a college community with a critical mass of its minorities, supportive communities within a college community, is clearly illustrated by my experience with Joseph. He was referred to me because he was on academic probation.

Joseph's mentor had been unable to contact him by phone—no phone number had been written on his application to the college. At the Registrar office I get a copy of his class schedule, and then go to his class as it's breaking up. I ask his teacher to point him out to me. I introduce myself, tell him why we need to talk, and we walk to my office.

Joseph is Native, age 23, self-contained. As we walk he's as indrawn as Bob Dylan on a rainy day at twilight. He's distant and I sense he perceives me as just one more authority about to tell him what he should do. When I meet him, in my mind he's Native American. By the end of our first meeting he's Native.

After very brief small talk in my office, I tell Joseph that during the summer I sent him a letter saying he was to be in the college Student Peer Mentoring Program, which was mandatory for all entering students on academic probation. I ask if he received the letter. He says he did. He asks, "Is my mentor Native?"

Through the years, I've mentored several Native students but no one has ever asked that question. I say, "I wish I had a Native student to mentor you but I don't."

When he speaks, Joseph is simply direct, not combative. "Should that be my problem or yours?"

After a speechless moment I answer, "You're right. There should be many more Native students at the college. I get what you're saying but all students on academic probation have to be in the program. You're in danger of losing your scholarship because of your grades. I don't want that to happen. I've received two early alerts."

"I'm willing to be in your program but I have to have a Native mentor."

I reach for a solution. "I'm not Native but given the circumstances, I could mentor you."

He looks at me as if I just don't get it. "Why do you think you would be able to connect with me well enough to mentor me? We have different priorities."

"No, I think our priorities are the same regarding school. We both want you to get a good education and graduate."

"I try to spend as much time as I can at the college but I have to divide my time. I'm one of my pueblo's dancers and that requires lots of practice, especially leading up to festivals. Sometimes I'm late to classes. I have many family obligations and sometimes I have to skip class altogether because of the needs of my pueblo."

"OK, that makes sense. I understand your circumstances are unique. I understand your culture and traditions are different, but in terms of mentoring you, we need to make this work for you. My mentoring program is very much about supporting each student's individuality, supporting their cultural traditions and timelines and respecting them. I created the program that way. I'm going to help you with scheduling your time because you have to go to your classes and get the education you're here for. You have to do the work, write the papers, and pass the exams."

After a long silence he says, "I'm here to study creative writing and I do want an education, but I'm not really comfortable, there aren't many Native students here. I don't have much in common with the other seven hundred. It didn't take me long to figure out that this college is mostly white professors teaching white students. If I didn't have a full scholarship I wouldn't want to be here at all. I'd be at the Institute of American Indian Arts. Do you know why there aren't more indigenous people here?"

I don't know the answer to his question. I search for an explanation but can't come up with anything worth explaining. "I know it's not enough, but I'm a member of the college's Diversity Committee and we're trying to increase the number of Native American, African-American, and Hispanic students, in fact all minorities at the college."

"You know, I'm not Native American, I'm Native. I'm indigenous. My people have always been here. So, what is your diversity committee doing to make the college more diverse?"

I answer, "We've talked with the president of the college and the head of Admissions and they both support a more diverse college."

"No disrespect meant, but you're an educator and my guess is you have no idea there is an Eight Northern Indian Pueblos Council about thirty miles from here." (Actually I do know that, having mentored Native students before.)

He looks directly at me. "Why doesn't somebody from your Diversity Committee open a discussion with the council's Higher Education Program? It should be a front burner issue at the college."

He's right. I tell him, "I'll call the council and ask if they'll allow me to speak about enrolling more Native students at the College of Santa Fe."

"Good," he replies, "that means a lot to me." He pauses, then says, "I'll help you mentor me." We shake hands.

Clearly, Joseph is a leader. On probation or not, he's brilliant, struggling with the hypocrisy of it all, living at cross purposes with his loyalties and his need for a good education.

The next day, mid-afternoon, he stops by my office and hands me a list of his pueblo's values. I read the list and tell him we'll use it as a guide for our mentoring.

Joseph's List:
- the concept of sharing is a major value in family life
- time is secondary to people and is seen more as a natural phenomenon
- nature is part of living and is part of happenings such as death, birth, and accidents
- acceptance of life is a style of being in harmony with the world
- family, including extended family, is of major importance, and the tribe and family to which one belongs provide significant meaning
- the basic worth of the individual is in terms of his or her family and tribe; individual responsibility is only a part of the total responsibility concept
- harmony and cooperative behavior are valued and encouraged
- tradition is important; it adds to the quality of life in the here-and-now
- assertive or aggressive behavior is seen as an impingement on other's dignity
- respect for elders is valued, and elders play an important part in family life

I tell Joseph I called the Eight Northern Indian Pueblos Council and the chairman invited me to the next meeting of the council's Higher Education Program to speak about how we could increase the number of Native students at the College of Santa Fe.

He's pleased. We talk about his classes, and when we discuss his creative nonfiction class, he says he's decided to write about our situation, with me unable to find a Native mentor for him. I tell him I like the idea.

THANK YOU FOR TAKING THIS FIRST STEP

Seated around a large table, I am the last to speak to the members of the Higher Education Program. I tell them I am employed by the College of Santa Fe and I asked to speak with them because a Native student at the college asked me to initiate talks aimed at enrolling more indigenous people.

After I speak, the chairman replies, "Thank you for coming and speaking on behalf of an Indian student. It has been many years since anyone from your college has shown any interest in how many Indian students attend the College of Santa Fe. Thank you for taking this first step. I ask that you tell your college president that the council is ready to meet, should the president wish to meet with us. You have my name and phone number. Your president can contact me if there is authentic interest in starting a dialogue that will lead to more Indian students at the College of Santa Fe."

I return to Santa Fe feeling hopeful, my spirit lifted. I was received by the council with great generosity of spirit and a sincere desire to expand the educational possibilities for their young people. Their commitment was inspiring.

Forthwith, I write a letter to our college president, reporting my meeting with educators from the Eight Northern Indian Pueblos Council Higher Education Program. I convey the council chairman's invitation to begin a dialogue at their next quarterly council meeting.

The following week I receive a note from our president stating "unequivocal support for the idea of more Native Americans at the college," but also stating that at this time he/she has decided not to meet with members of the Higher Education Program.

I have a sinking feeling in my stomach. There's got to be a mistake. This is supposed to be the president of a college, theoretically an intelligent, enlightened person, not just another politician playing to moneyed constituencies. At my urging, the Diversity Committee writes a letter to the college president asking him/her to reconsider. The president declines to do so.

I'm embarrassed and offended by the president's cavalier non-response to the council's gracious invitation. It was an honor and an opportunity to be invited by the council to begin discussions. The College of Santa Fe could have worked with them to raise money for scholarships. There were initiatives we could have developed, including classes in Native Studies, an area of study perhaps overseen by an endowed Chair.

It's a difficult task telling Joseph what happened, but when I do he doesn't seem surprised, having had to live with this concept of token diversity all his life.

TO DANCE IS TO PRAY

The week before midterms, Joseph stops by my office and hands me a paper he wrote for his creative writing class. He says, "This paper describes the meaning of dance for me and my tribe. It's a window to the education most important to us—our traditions and experience of spirit."

With permission, an excerpt from Joseph's paper, "To Dance is to Pray."

"The meaning of the dance for me is my connection through the drum to the heartbeat of the earth. All cultures have always had a drum. It has always been representative of the heartbeat of the earth mother. And along with that comes the dance. It is a natural evolution of people to dance to the rhythm of the drum, no matter what tribe, no matter what nation, no matter what continent.

"It's all about connection to the drum. Native people don't dance to music. They embody the music and they allow the rhythm and the energy of the drum and the earth to feed their body into the dance. When people are truly connected, it's a place that really sets the spirit free.

"In today's culture, when we have so many things that we need to do to survive—our jobs, our schooling, all these things that we need to do—we're living in two worlds. We're trying to hold on to a culture while living in one that doesn't fit, one that doesn't teach connection, one that doesn't teach community and holding one another's hands in advance of beauty, grace, love and welcoming. So it is important for all people to try to find connections. That's what pow wow is really about. The core of it is about people connecting. And that's what the dance is.

"To dance is to pray, to pray is to live, to live is to heal. It's a circle of life. The dance is always in a circle. You will see people dance in a clockwise direction in most pow wows. It's a way of dancing with the sun, dancing with the energy of the rotation of the earth.

"Our ways are not about domination. Our ways are about harmony. For me, that is in my dance."

Joseph passes all his classes and is no longer on academic probation. I feel I've gained as much as he has.

A WELCOMING COMMUNITY FOR EVERYONE

Students arrive at college without community, having left whatever form of it they had in their home town, or in Joseph's case, pueblo. Loss of community can have consequences similar to loss of a spiritual center. We are a community-forming species. Some students seek community in diverse gatherings such as college clubs, dorm rooms, classes, and on-campus activities. Others prefer to interact with those who most closely mirror themselves—their background, beliefs, traditions. Either way, students seek a sense of belonging and identity, social supports for academic success.

College communities should be designed to create a welcoming academic and social community, one comprising meaningful numbers of students from many races, cultures, and beliefs. This allows students to interact with the college community at large, and, if they wish, find their sub-community, their way home away from home.

Social bonds formed in a diverse college community can provide powerful support for students struggling to achieve academic goals. Colleges should be consciously crafted communities with a critical mass of minorities, enough so every student can find a personal connection with a group of peers who take them in.

Without diversity, under-represented students may under-achieve because they feel alienated from the groups that form the majority of students.

Dismayed and affected by what happened between the council and the college, I now take additional steps to ensure that minority students in the mentoring program are connected to culturally relevant support from their community, even if that community support is in part virtual, created online. I do the same for students belonging to a majority grouping, be it social, ethnic, racial, or technological.

My training of program supervisors and mentors has also been affected, with increased importance given to culturally sensitive mentoring.

Joseph shaped the way I mentored him that semester. When we met in my office, after discussing his academic life, our conversations turned to his life in tribal community. He talked about the shoulders of his ancestors upon which he stood. I was honored that he shared as much as he did with me, and respectful when he said he'd rather not discuss a subject.

Through my interactions with Joseph, the Eight Northern Indian Pueblos Council Higher Education Program, and the administration at the College of Santa Fe, I gained insight into how educational institutions, through a lack of awareness and planning, can unintentionally create an uninviting educational environment for students, often minority students and students with a disability. The result? These students may slip through the cracks of a one-size-fits-all education that lacks personal relevance for them.

It is important for educational institutions to welcome minority and disability students as valuable members of a diverse, supportive community, with a critical mass of each minority. This leads to enriched education for all students.

My training of program supervisors and mentors now includes a more in-depth discussion about culturally sensitive mentoring that is responsive to a mentee's history—their ancestry and family life, their culture, embodied or rejected beliefs, values, and traditions manifesting as their life today.

THE INSTITUTE OF AMERICAN INDIAN ARTS

I was asked by the Institute of American Indian Arts in Santa Fe to give a day-long workshop for Native educational leaders. My workshop, "Building Mentoring Programs," explored how to create or enrich existing mentoring programs.

We started the workshop by introducing ourselves, talking about mentors we've had over the years who have helped us with our struggles. Deep gratitude for their mentors was present in each who spoke, and the life-altering support of mentoring became increasingly clear.

During my workshop, participants, almost all Native, talked about the rapid changes taking place in their communities, especially with young people. We discussed the influence of mass media, particularly the Internet and television, and they expressed how antithetical the media's culture is to many Native values.

I talked about how to develop mentoring programs designed to address their communities' most threatening problems, which they identified as lack of opportunity and hope, unemployment, drug and alcohol abuse, and a high youth suicide rate.

My workshop explored how to create Seven-Day Plans for mentored students, designed to help them achieve their potential each week for their minds, bodies, and spirits. I suggested that their mentoring programs, created for Native students, should draw on their Native community's strengths, especially tribe and family, cultural beliefs, traditions, and values.

Throughout the day we shared stories within stories, the shoulders upon which we all stand today.

EPILOGUE

MENTORING POTENTIAL

It has been said, "The past is prologue." While this may be true in many arenas of life, it doesn't necessarily hold true for human potential. Most humans are conditioned to believe that their self-perceptions, drawn largely from the past, are inevitable indicators of future potential. All too often this becomes a self-fulfilling prophecy, ending in under-achievement or failure.

What is our potential when we rely on our ego, fear, and competition to motivate us and guide our everyday thoughts and actions? What is our potential when we call upon spirit to guide us? What is our human potential for mind, body and spirit?

How do we mentor human potential in our daily lives, in our communities and schools? By living a life of love and service that gently breaks down the self-defining, self-limiting, self containers that prevent us from living with conscious awareness of our unique place in our infinitely mysterious universe.

We mentor our human potential by living with humility and awe, the only appropriate response to our existence in a cosmic crucible of time, space, and matter whose scale dwarfs the human imagination.

Mentoring our potential we mentor our potential to love and be loved, to serve others, to live with gratitude and humility, interdependently and independently. We examine our conditioned cultural goals, which in our capitalist, material world usually center on money, status, and the "good" things in life (not that there's anything wrong with them). It's just that our potential as humans for an experience of our deepest humanity, a noble goal, requires an awareness and practice of living each day for our communal and personal highest good: mind, body, and spirit in synergistic, life-affirming harmony and balance.

Our human potential is the potential to experience and celebrate all existence, higher states of consciousness, love unchained from fear, our oneness experienced on a daily basis. Our potential puts us in relationship with the dynamic energies of the universe expressed through each of its living beings.

Most college students are distracted from the stunning miracle of their existence by their ego-bound perception of life limited in scope and scale to their college campus. Many of these students have lost their sense of wonder and it is in wonder that we discover our most dynamic human potential.

The world will never starve for want of wonders but only for want of wonder.—G. K. Chesterton

To nurture your mentees' potential, nurture their dreams and celebrate the miracle of our shared existence. Help them live their lives with spirit, whatever path or belief that might turn out to be.

CREATE A REVOLUTION OF SPIRIT

I believe all levels of education should have holistically-shaped student peer mentoring programs that help participants achieve their academic, social, and spiritual potential.

Peers can help peers in a way no one else can. They understand each other from the inside, sharing the same generation, the same culture within the culture at large, the same heroes and villains, fears and hopes. They're on the same side of the digital divide, affected by the same music and media, the same global and local cruelties, the same opportunities and threats to survival. Peers at academic risk are often helped most by successful peers who can light the way.

Student peer mentoring with spirit in our schools at all levels is a revolution waiting to happen. Mentors can help speed this revolution by mentoring holistically, with spirit as an ally in the trenches of education. Help spread this peaceful, deeply human revolution. Create a holistic student peer mentoring program. Start a revolution of service and achievement. We are One. Let the revolution begin.

For information about Scott Seldin's workshop training for Student Peer Mentoring Program supervisors and mentors, and/or his academic and personal development coaching, visit www.mentoringhumanpotential.com or call (505) 466-2878.

Quick Reference

You are welcome to print any forms and checklists shown below:

PRINTABLE FORMS AND CHECKLISTS

In addition, the reader may be interested in reviewing the following tables and lists:

Sources

Capra, Fritjof. *The Tao of Physics*. New York: Bantam Books, Inc., 2000

Ellis, Dave. *Becoming a Master Student*. Boston, New York: Houghton Mifflin Company, 2009.

Gardener, Howard. *Frames of Mind*. New York: Basic Books, 1983.

Lama, Dalai. *Ethics for the New Millennium*. New York: Riverhead Books, 1999.

Lovato, Andrew. *Santa Fe Hispanic Culture: Preserving Identity in a Tourist Town*. Albuquerque, New Mexico: University of New Mexico Press, 2004.

Mann, Thomas. *The Magic Mountain*. New York: Alfred A. Knopf, Inc., 1927.

Maslow, Abraham. *Toward a Psychology of Being*. New York: John Wiley & Sons, Inc., 1999.

Mitchell, Stephen. *Tao Te Ching*. New York: Harper Perennial, 1991.

Novak, John. *How to Meditate*. Nevada City, CA: Crystal Clarity Publishers, 1994.

Smith, Huston. *Beyond the Post-Modern Mind*. New York: The Crossroad Publishing Company, 1982.

Tolle, Eckhart. *The Power of Now*. Lovato, CA: New World Library, 1999.

Wong, Linda. *Essential Study Skills*. Boston, New York: Houghton Mifflin Co., 2003.

Zubizarreta, John. *The Learning Portfolio*. Bolton, MA: Anker Publishing Company, Inc., 2004.